TIME-SLIP

Time-Slip

JOHANNES VON BUTTLAR

Translated by Nicholas Fry

SIDGWICK & JACKSON

LONDON

First published in Great Britain in 1978 by
Sidgwick and Jackson Limited

Originally published in West Germany in 1977 by
C. Bertelsmann Ver-lag under the title Zeitsprung

This translation © *1978 by Sidgwick and Jackson Limited*

ISBN 0 283 98505 4

Printed in Gt. Britain by Caledonian Graphics Ltd.
London & Cumbernauld
for Sidgwick and Jackson Limited
1 Tavistock Chambers, Bloomsbury Way
London WC1A 2SG

Phototypesetting by Rainbow Graphics, Liverpool

FOR LINCHEN

FRAGMENT

They say: the breadth and the length,
The depth – and by this they mean
Within our earthly limits
The geometry of three.

Unified, three-fold space
Welded in crystalline forms,
Meekly splits in our dreaming,
Where not even time performs

Then all of a sudden to live
In the shadowy mirror of time,
Out of the fifth dimension
On an extragalactic cloud nine.

You say: its beyond comprehension . . .

JOHANNES VON GUENTHER

Contents

1

Countdown

---

4 January 1974
The control room at Vandenberg Air Force Base in California.

Technicians and officers gaze tensely out at a Minuteman
missile ready for firing.

Numbers light up on telemetric equipment. The radar is
on. The countdown is running.

...3 ...2 ...1 ...0

The Minuteman lifts off. The stages ignite according to
plan. Everything is functioning perfectly. The figures tumble
past on the digital counters in the control room, providing
data on height, speed and the state of the missile. The experts
relax and follow the flight on their radar screens. A laser
tracking device is switched on. A couple of officers follow the
flight path with their field-glasses.

Now the last stage ignites. The Minuteman's flight path
dips, according to plan. Everyone sees it, including the
technicians and the radar team at their screens.

But suddenly it's no longer there. The Minuteman is gone.
Vanished. Disappeared without a trace.

There's an astonished silence in the control room.

9

Finally a bewildered voice says: 'I don't believe it! It's not possible! The thing can't just vanish into thin air!'

'The unarmed Minuteman warhead ought to be coming down by now,' says another, speaking everyone's thoughts.

'Okay, so a warhead can get lost. But not like this. It can't just vanish,' exclaims one of the officers. 'And what happened to the radar contact? It's just not possible. It's unreal.'

'Not a trace. Nothing. Vanished. It's a nightmare,' murmurs the technician at the telemetric equipment. 'The crate was functioning perfectly. It's incomprehensible. But we can't all be dreaming.'

'One moment,' said the researcher, interrupting the conversation. 'Our subject is dreaming.'

'How can you be so sure?' asked the journalist.

'You can see it from the variation in the brain waves which is showing up on this recorder.' The scientist pointed to the electroencephalograph as he spoke.

The control panel of the EEG equipment looked like something out of the cockpit of a jumbo jet. A jumble of cables led from the complex assemblage of hardware into the next room, where a sleeping figure lay isolated behind a soundproof glass panel. The multicoloured wires were connected to small metal plates attached to the sleeper's head.

In the darkened room, the dreaming figure seemed like some fabulous beast with outstretched tentacles.

'It is not so long since our knowledge in this field was fundamentally altered,' the scientist went on. 'In fact it was only in 1953 that the researches of Professor Nathaniel Kleitman finally disposed of the traditional theories about dreaming. Until then it had been the generally held view that dreams were a fleeting, momentary event, brought on by indigestion, a full bladder or a sudden extraneous noise. A deep, dreamless sleep, begun long before midnight, was held to be the best recipe for good health. It was a view held even by those who considered that dreams had some psychological or prophetic significance. Even the specialist literature had nothing better to offer. Nor could it explain why many people can remember having dreamed practically every night, while others maintain that they never dream at all. The whole thing was a mystery.

'But 1953 was the turning point. And as is so often the case with scientific discoveries, it happened by chance. Kleitman was carrying out sleep experiments with a large number of infants in the Department of Physiology at Chicago University. During the course of the experiments, one of his collaborators noticed that a baby's eyes were making rapid, jerking movements under the closed lids. The observation aroused Kleitman's attention.

'As a result of this discovery, the sleep experiments were extended to adults. The researchers wanted to know if they would also show rapid eye movements, and if so to establish their cause.

'The adults were placed under direct observation. The research workers actually stood, bent over the subjects, and watched. They did observe periodic abrupt eye movements under the sleepers' closed lids. But observation was a laborious business and no one research worker could continue it for long. Another means of observation had to be found.

'Kleitman and his assistants hit upon the idea of observing the sleeping subjects by means of an electroencephalograph or EEG. This is a machine which measures the electrical currents produced by the brain. Small metal plates called electrodes are attached to the subject's head where they pick up the electrical impulses of the brain and transmit them via cables to the EEG machine. Here they are amplified millions of times and transformed into visible marks by a pen on a roll of paper. The jagged lines produced represent the brain waves of the subject.

'The same method can be used to record the electrical impulses of the eyes. As soon as the eyeballs move during sleep, electrodes attached to the closed lids pick up these impulses and transmit them to the EEG recorder. The result is known as an electro-oculogram – like this one here.'

The scientist pointed to the EEG recorder and continued:

'You want to write about dreams. But do you know why you're taking an interest in them?'

'Yes and no,' the journalist answered. 'What I really want to do is investigate reality. To go back to the Minuteman, for example – its disappearance was a reality, wasn't it? Something which actually happened?'

'Of course. There can be no doubt about that. But you haven't heard the end of the story yet. It's more like the reality, or if you like the unreality, of a dream. Take a look at our sleeper here. Now, while he's dreaming, he is living in another reality. Did you know, by the way, that everyone dreams, even if they can't remember doing so?

'In many respects, dreams are a special area of experience. They occur in a state of what one might call "total privacy". The dreamer has laid aside all inhibitions, for in the dream world there are no obligations or taboos. Dreams come without advance warning, they are involuntary and un-influenced by the dreamer's will. The sleeper cannot direct the visions of his dream world, as the waking man can direct his ideas and thoughts. His is an autonomously created reality, which unfolds like a play or a film. He is simultaneously producer, actor and audience in a private drama. He hears and speaks, smells and sees things in colour. His senses are alert and ready to respond to any stimulus.

'In a dream, everything seems natural and real, whether the dreamer is witnessing his own burial, or is reborn and becomes a child again. Everything is possible. He can fall into an abyss but remain unharmed. He can fly or float in the air, do things which would be impossible if he were awake. He

seems familiar with men and places which he has never seen
in his life before. He is a time-traveller, with access to both
past and future. For the dreamer, that which he dreams is
reality, something which actually happens. It is life in
another dimension. But his experiences in his dream life will
be the same as they would in a similar situation if he was
awake. Even in a dream, for instance, he will feel uncomfor-
table at having to appear naked in public. And he will run
away from a bear in panic. But even "unrealistic" dreams
have a verisimilitude which seems to indicate that they must
be the reflection of a deeper, more basic reality than we ever
dream of in our waking moments.

'Dreams are a universal phenomenon. Everyone dreams
every night, and as we now know, continuously through the
night as well. Sleep, dreams and death are the ultimate rulers
of our existence. Even our strongest drives – hunger and
love – are overcome by sleep and dreams. No one is
spared – infant or grandmother, worker, manager, bus-
driver or astronaut. They all sleep, and they all dream.'

'Did I hear you say that each of us dreams every night, and
according to the latest discoveries, throughout the period in
which we are asleep?' The journalist looked curiously at the
sleeping subject and turned to the scientist as he continued:
'How can you tell that? How do you know when a person is
dreaming, and how long the dream lasts?'

'Your last question about the duration of a dream reminds
me of Maury's famous guillotine dream,' replied the
researcher. 'Louis Ferdinand Alfred Maury was French and
lived at the end of the last century. The first attempts at a
modern, systematic investigation of dreams began with him.
He once dreamed that he had been dragged before a
revolutionary tribunal, tried by Robespierre and Marat and
condemned to death on the guillotine. He was taken to the
scaffold, shackled to a board by the executioner, and behead-
ed. He felt the guillotine blade slice his head from his

shoulders – and at that point he woke up. What had happened was that the headboard of the bed had fallen and landed
on the back of his neck.

'This dream caused violent controversy. Arguments raged,
particularly in the columns of the contemporary *Revue
Philosophique,* as to how it was possible to dream so many
details in the few fractions of a second which elapsed between
the collapse of the bed-head and his waking up. One of the
favourite explanations was that in a dream everything
happens at lightning speed. However, the most modern data
do not support this theory of a "split-second dream". In
fact the most up-to-date research suggests that Maury's
guillotine dream was not really a dream at all, but a latent
idea, which was activated by the blow on the back of the
neck.

'So you can see that a relatively short time ago, people had
a very different idea of the duration of dreams from that
which they have today. Thanks to the latest monitoring
techniques, today's dream researchers can more or less
establish the duration of a dream. In addition to the
measurements of electrical currents in the brain and eye
movement, all the other reactions and movements of our
sleeping subject are recorded here also. The characteristic
movements of a sleeping body, the smallest twitching of
limbs, fingers or toes, such as you see now' – the scientist
indicated the sleeper – 'are recorded by an electromyogram.
Even erections are indicated. At the same time heart activity
is monitored by an electrocardiogram, while an electro-
dermatogram indicates the state of dryness or moisture of the
skin. Breathing is checked by a respirograph. But even with
all these technical resources, the simplest method is still to
wake the sleeping person and ask him directly what he has
dreamed. The results are often surprising. In the course of my
research I came across some puzzling circumstances which
may possibly help to explain our present experiment. In my

opinion, it is a space-time problem, like that of the Minuteman.'

'If I'm to follow you, you must first of all tell me what happened to the vanished Minuteman.'

'It turned up again,' said the researcher, looking pensively at the journalist.

'Not until three days later, but in precisely the same spot where it had disappeared seventy-two hours earlier. That is amazing enough in itself, but it's not the whole story. I'm sure you know that caesium atomic clocks are placed at various strategic points on the earth's surface, for example on the Pacific island of Kwajalein, which is one of the Marshall Islands, in the US state of Maryland and in Canada, to name but a few. These atomic clocks are a marvel of technical precision. They are the most accurate instrument for measuring time which exists, varying by no more than a millionth of a second per year. Also these caesium atomic clocks are all synchronized with one another.

'When the Minuteman suddenly disappeared, the atomic clock on Kwajalein suddenly jumped out of synchrony. This is something completely unheard-of for a caesium clock, a paradoxical event which just can't happen. But it did. At the moment the Minuteman disappeared, the Kwajalein clock jumped 1.1 microseconds. But when the Minuteman reappeared after three days in the same place, the atomic clock fell back into synchrony with all the other caesium clocks.

'Perhaps you think I dreamed all this up, but you'd be wrong. The American author Martin Caidin reports the occurrence in his book, *Three Corners to Nowhere*.'

The scientist shrugged and turned back to his monitoring instruments.

'I'm beginning to see what you're driving at,' said the journalist. 'Basically, you're engaged in the search for reality, just like I am. Or, to put it another way, you believe that the disappearance of the Minuteman has a direct connection with the time-shift of the atomic clock on Kwajalein. It looks to me as though there was an alteration in the space/time continuum for some reason or other, and for a certain period, which was responsible for its disappearance.'

'Right,' answered the researcher. 'There are two or three possible ways in which our space/time continuum can be altered. One is physical, through acceleration or gravitation, as Einstein demonstrated by his theory of relativity; another is psychological, the kind which is revealed in the phenomenon of dreaming. And this brings us back to the notion of reality, which is linked to our concept of space and time. The first type of reality is that the Minuteman disappeared from our space/time continuum in broad daylight, for seventy-two hours. The second is our sleeping subject. In his dream-space/time places and events arise out of nothing.

'All our perceptions and experiences, everything which we see, constitute an event in space and time. Everything which happens – including our own existence – has a certain duration in time. Such is the way we see things that nothing can exist for us without space and time. But this has nothing whatsoever to do with the calendar, or our measurement of time by a clock. Time exists independently of clocks.

'Thus reality for us means a particular perception of an event in space and time. And on closer investigation, we will find that the first form of reality affects the second in an almost unreal fashion.'

2

The Second Reality

The court in the Westphalian town of Paderborn was filled to bursting point. In the dock sat a teenager, flanked by two policemen. He was thirteen years old, and he was deathly pale, but apart from this he looked very much like any other schoolboy of that age. He certainly didn't look like a murderer. Yet it was murder that he was accused of.

The youth had strangled the daughter of a neighbour, who had been his playmate for years, with a gauze bandage, and then stabbed her brutally with a kitchen knife. The crowd followed the proceedings in stunned silence.

The young murderer had been questioned by psychologists and a number of interesting facts had come to light. He claimed that three days before the murder he had had a terrible dream. His friend had passed by his parents' house on the way home from school and he had called her in to show her some pictures. Once she was inside he had leaped upon her, throttled her with a gauze bandage and then stabbed at her savagely with a kitchen knife. Then his parents had arrived and the dream had ended.

The youth confessed that three days later, when the girl

passed by outside, he had been overcome by an irresistible urge to act out the dream.

In Bayonne, in south-west France, the young wife of a plumber was woken up by the sound of her husband cursing violently in his sleep. She tried to shake him awake, murmuring soothing words, but he raged on, oblivious. She watched in helpless desperation as he jumped out of bed, climbed onto the window sill and leaped from the fifth storey of the block of flats.

An office worker appeared in the police station in Constantine, Algeria, in a hysterical state, and confessed to having murdered his wife and two children. He could give no explanation for the deed, and kept desperately repeating how much he loved his family.

The police drove him straight back to the scene of the crime, and were amazed to find the man's family all alive and well. The wife was merely worried because her husband had left the house unusually early in the morning, and she had not seen him since.

It turned out that the office worker had had such a vivid dream that he was convinced he had actually murdered his family. Hardly knowing what he was doing, he had gone to the police to give himself up.

The French psychologist and author Raymond de Becker commented on these episodes in his book *Les Machinations de la Nuit*:

'For me, the remarkable thing about these dreams is the fragility of the frontier which divides dream from what is generally called reality. It is reminiscent of the attitude which primitive peoples have towards their dreams: for them things which happen in dreams are as real as things which happen in everyday life. It's the classic story of the Negro chief who dreamed that he made a journey to England, and the next morning was greeted with a homecoming ceremony by his tribe.'

In the same way, the office worker in Constantine carried the reality of his dream over into the reality of everyday life. The teenager in Paderborn felt compelled to act out the experience he had had in a dream. And the plumber in Bayonne leaped to his death under the influence of a dream whose contents are unknown to us. The distinguishing feature of all these cases is that one form of reality became extended into another.

Fortunately not all dreams have such a dramatic outcome, but even so we cannot be sure how far our actions are affected or predetermined by dreams. At any rate, modern psychoanalysis confirms that our behaviour is closely linked with the phenomenon of dreaming, and interestingly enough, this view goes right back to the origins of mankind. The so-called primitive cultures, like those of the Australian aborigines and the North American Indians, possessed a remarkable store of psychological knowledge which was largely intuitive, albeit often linked with barbaric customs. A typical example are the Iroquois Indians.

The Iroquois were a group of North American Indian tribes speaking related languages, about 35,000 of whose descendants now live in reservations in the USA and about 15,000 in protected areas in Canada. They originally lived east of the Mississippi, in the region of Lakes Eyrie and Ontario and on the lower St Lawrence River. They had a reputation as bold and fearsome warriors, unswayed by feeling and indifferent to pain. Five of the Iroquois tribes – the Mohawk, Oneida,

Onodaga, Cayuga and Seneca – joined together in the Iroquois Confederacy, which was constantly at war with the Hurons who also spoke an Iroquois language. When the first white immigrants arrived at the beginning of the seventeenth century, they were still living a primitive, hunter's existence. They were considered the most intelligent of the North American Indians and were not only the terror of the other native tribes, but also played an important role in the history of North America.

We owe our knowledge of the customs and mode of life of the Iroquois chiefly to early reports made by Jesuit missionaries between 1611 and 1768 to their superiors in Paris and Quebec. They give a very clear picture of the behaviour of these hunter tribes, who despite their outward barbarism maintained a very high level of morality. The Jesuit fathers lived among the Indians, learned their language and observed their customs very much at first hand. The Iroquois had a strict code of ethics, which demanded generosity, strong tribal consciousness and a sense of duty towards the community. Strictly speaking they had only one god, the god of dreams. They obeyed him unconditionally and followed the 'signs' which he sent them in sleep in every detail.

As an example, an Iroquois dreamed during the night that he had taken a bath. As soon as he awoke, he ran round his village from hut to hut, making each of his tribal brothers pour a bucket of water over him – undaunted by the fact that it was icy cold. There are various other cases of Iroquois dreaming that they had bought a dog in Quebec. In each instance, they actually made the 150-mile journey to fetch the 'dream dog' from the capital.

The Jesuit reports also mention other, less edifying dreams. A warrior hacked off one of his fingers, for example, because he had dreamed that his enemy cut off his finger while he was taking him prisoner.

In the middle of the seventeenth century, the Jesuit father

Fremin reported that the Iroquois were convinced that it was a crime to ignore the promptings of a single dream. They believed that they would die if they did not carry out the orders they received while dreaming.

'They think of nothing else, they speak of nothing else, and their huts are filled with their dreams,' wrote Fremin.

One warrior had himself dragged, stark naked and shackled, through his village in obedience to an order he had received in a dream. Another dreamed that his hut had burned down and so his hut was ceremonially burned in reality. In 1642 a Huron dreamed that he had been taken prisoner by an alien tribe. The elders of his tribe held a council to discuss how to avoid this misfortune, and it was decided that the unfortunate warrior should be burned to death.

Every year at the end of February, the Iroquois celebrated their 'festival of dreams', which lasted three to four days. Men, women and children ran around naked, often wearing masks and coloured paints. They would run like madmen from one hut to another, creating havoc and smashing everything which got in their way. They drenched their fellow tribesmen with hot water or threw cold ashes over them. Everyone had dreamed something, and on entering a hut he would stay there until someone else had guessed his dream and turned it into action. The guesser had to procure the object which the other had dreamed of, for the latter's life depended on it.

In 1958 the American anthropologist Dr Anthony F. C. Wallace of the University of Pennsylvania wrote a study of the Iroquois dream cult. He found startling similarities between the dream theories of the Indians and those of the father of psychoanalysis, Sigmund Freud (1856–1939). For the Iroquois – just as for Freud – dreams were the means of expression of the soul. A dream for them signified a wish to be fulfilled, it was the expression of an individual's wishes in a language unique to that person.

Wallace writes:

> Intuitively, the Iroquois had achieved a great degree of
> psychological sophistication. They recognized conscious
> and unconscious parts of the mind. They knew the great
> force of unconscious desires, and were aware that the
> frustration of these desires could cause mental and physical
> ('psychosomatic') illness. They understood that these
> desires were expressed in symbolic form by dreams, but
> that the individual could not always properly interpret
> these dreams himself. They had noted the distinction
> between the manifest and latent content of dreams, and
> employed what sounds like the technique of free associa-
> tion to uncover the latent meaning. And they considered
> that the best method for the relief of psychic and psycho-
> somatic distress was to give the frustrated desire satisfac-
> tion, either directly or symbolically.

The Digueno Indians of southern California use a technique
of dream therapy which is amazingly similar to the treatment
of dreams in Western psychotherapy. When a Digueno has a
sexual problem, he seeks out his shaman, the medicine man.
The latter persuades the patient to talk about his dreams and
his sex life, both real and imagined. The shaman begins his
therapy by asserting that it is senseless for the patient to
conceal anything, since he knows all the latter's dreams in
advance. Often the sick man is put into a mild hypnotic
trance, to enable him to talk without inhibitions. Afterwards
the shaman discusses the patient's fantasies and sex-life with
him, then bleeds him and prescribes a special diet. If he is
single, he is advised to get married, so that he can fulfil his
fantasies through real experience.

The shaman's tribal functions not only include that of
doctor. As the witch-doctor he is also the mediator between
the world of spirits, the souls of the departed, and his fellow

tribesmen. By the use of particular ecstatic techniques he can put himself into a trance in which his body becomes rigid, setting his soul free to travel to the world of dreams. While dreaming he makes contact with the souls of the tribe's ancestors, and with all kinds of spirits and gods.

According to the theories of the English anthropologist Sir Edward Tylor (1832–1917), who was world-famous in his own time, primitive peoples were puzzled by two biological mysteries – first by the difference between living and dead bodies, and secondly by the figures which appeared in dreams and visions. According to Tylor, the 'primitive philosopher' inferred that in addition to his real existence, every human being also led a phantom life, and had a 'ghost' which was a being separated from his physical body. In the conceptual world of the 'primitive thinker', this inevitably led to the uniting of both forms of the existence – the real and the unreal – in a single being. This being could come to men while they were awake in the form of a vision, and while they were asleep as a dream, and was their ghostly double, separated from the body. According to Tylor, the 'primitive thinker' deduced from this concept the idea of life after death.

It is on this succession of concepts – dream, death and continued existence after death – that shamanism also is based. Shamanism goes back to the beginnings of humanity, and is the basis of all mythologies and religions. Widely distributed throughout the world, it is upheld with equal conviction by its different adherents, even though they are geographically and ethnically far apart from one another.

The instruction of novices in shamanism takes place in dreams, since it is only in dreams that real time is abolished and replaced by a mythical time. Thus the shaman takes part in the beginning of the world and in creation. The so-called dream of initiation usually takes place in childhood.

According to shamanistic belief, the shaman experiences his first initiation dream inside the mother's body. The embryo is said to begin dreaming as early as the fifth month of pregnancy, and amazingly enough this view is now being confirmed by the latest scientific discoveries. According to the shamans, embryos dream about their growth and forthcoming birth. They alternate between sleep and waking and know when their mother goes to sleep, shortly afterwards going to sleep themselves. There are even common elements in the mother's dreams and those of her unborn child, but they have their origin in neither. Like all other dreams they come from a second, external reality. Also, the unborn child closely follows his mother's actions. The potential shaman has a fundamental desire not to be born. He dreams of killing himself and his mother by turning sideways in the mother's body. Although shamanism is inherited, the future shaman only becomes qualified when he has learned the rules of initiation in a dream, in which he is taught the shaman's way of life and taboos by his ancestors, and by the gods and spirits.

A Siberian shaman novice dreamed that he had smallpox and was unconscious for three days. Since he was apparently dead, he was almost buried alive on the third day. But in fact, it was during this period that his initiation took place. He remembered being carried into the middle of a lake, where he was addressed by the Black Death with the words:

'The lords of the water bestow on you the gift of shamanism. Your shaman name is buottarie (=diver).'

With these words the plague whipped up the waters of the lake and the novice shot up out of the water, left the lake and climbed a mountain. There he was met by a naked woman, and began to drink at her breast.

'I suckle you because you are my child,' said the woman. She was the mistress of the waters. 'You will have to overcome many difficulties and life will be very hard for you.'

From the lord of the underworld, the husband of the

mistress of the waters, the novice received two guides, an ermine and a mouse. The two of them led him to the underworld, where his guides showed him seven tents with torn roofs. In the first the novice found the inhabitants of the underworld and the lords of smallpox. They tore his heart out of his body and threw it into a cooking pot. In the other tents lived the lord of insanity, the lords of nervous illness and the bad shamans. In this way the novice received knowledge of all the illnesses which afflict mankind.

After this, his companions led him to the land of the shamans, who taught him how to use his throat and voice. From there he was taken to the banks of the nine lakes. In the middle of the lakes was an island, and in the middle of this a young birch tree rose high into the sky. It was the tree of the lord of the earth (the tree of the world). Around it nine different plants were growing, and these were the ancestors of all earthly plants. The surrounding lakes were each inhabited by a species of bird, all different kinds of ducks, a swan and a sparrow-hawk. The novice visited all the lakes. A few were salty, while others were so hot that he could not approach their banks.

When he had seen everything he raised his head and saw at the top of the tree people of many different races: Samoyeds, Russians, Dolgans, Yakuts and Tungus.

He heard voices saying, 'It has been decided to give you a tambourine from the branches of the tree.'

When the novice was about to fly away with the lords of the lake, and moved away from the bank, the lord of the tree called out: 'One of my branches has just broken off, take it with you and make a drum out of it, it should serve you your whole life long.'

The lord of the tree also ordered him to make three drums out of the three forks of the branch. Three women were to watch over these, and each of the three drums was to be used in a particular ceremony. The first was for shamanizing women in childbed, the second was to be used for healing the sick, and the third was for finding people who were lost in the snow. The lord of the tree also gave a branch to all the other men in the tree-top. But then he showed himself in human form down to the chest and called out, 'There is one branch which I will not give to the shamans, and which must belong to the rest of mankind. They can build houses out of it or use it for something else. I am the tree which gives life to all men.'

The novice clutched his branch and was about to fly away with it when he heard another voice. This revealed to him the healing powers of seven plants, instructed him in the art of shamanizing and ordered him to marry three wives. (Later he actually married three orphans, whom he had cured of smallpox.)

He flew on and came to a lake of infinite size. There he found some trees and seven stones which spoke to him in turn. The first had teeth like a bear and was hollowed out like a basket. It told him that it was the stone of gravity and lent its weight to the fields so that the wind should not carry them away. The second stone served for smelting iron. The novice stayed with the stones for seven days, in order to learn from them how they could be useful to mankind.

Next the ermine and the mouse led him to a high, round mountain. He saw an opening, and went through, into a brilliantly lit cavern. All around was reflecting glass, and in the middle something shone like fire. Then he realized that it was not a fire burning, but light penetrating through an opening in the roof.

After leaving the cavern he came to a desert and saw a mountain range in the far distance. When he finally reached it after three days, he found a way up it and came upon a naked man working a pair of bellows. Hanging over a fire was a cauldron 'as big as half the earth'. When the naked man saw the novice, he reached for him with an enormous pair of tongs, and the novice had just time to think, 'I am dead.'

The naked man struck off his head, dismembered his body and threw everything into the cauldron. There it cooked for three years on end.

The naked man hammered the head of the novice on the third of three anvils. This was the anvil on which the best shamans are forged. Next the smith threw the head into one of three water butts. This was the one which held the coldest water. At the same time he told the novice that there would be no point in using his shaman's magic if he was summoned to a sick man and the water was already very hot, for such a man would already be lost. If the water was lukewarm, the sick man would get well, while cold water was the sign of health.

The smith now fished the novice's bones out of the river, put them together and covered them with flesh. Then he counted them and noticed that there were three left over. So he bade the novice make three shaman's costumes. He forged the head of the novice and explained to him how the letters inside (i.e. the thoughts) must be read. He exchanged his eyes for a pair of mythical ones, so that he would see through these, and not through his own, fleshly eyes, while he was shamanizing. Finally he pierced holes for his ears, so that he would understand the language of the plants. Now the shaman found himself once more on top of a high mountain and finally woke up in his yurt amongst his own people. From now on he could shamanize and sing without ever tiring.

One of the recurrent features of shamanism is the striving to master the cycle of life, birth and rebirth with the help of dreams. As a 'newly forged man', the shaman believes that he can overcome the material boundaries of existence – that he can repeal the physical laws and reach into the very structure of the universe. It is this possibility which dreams offer.

In shamanism the consciousness of the individual is

deliberately trained towards accepting as natural the influence of intangible forces. The shaman's drum bears a
symbolic representation of a man's journey through the
middle of the three worlds. The sounding of the 'primeval
note' on the drum brings everything into harmony so that
ecstasy can be achieved. Now the journey to the world of
dreams can be consciously experienced.

For the Australian aborigines, creation is 'the eternal
dream-time', with which earthly history is inextricably
linked. Thus the whole world is the dream of a conscious
dreamer, a dream in which the different planes of reality
merge into one another.

Dreaming played a central and dominant role in the life of
the early cultures. Its significance for them was chiefly
symbolic and they often showed astounding psychological
insight in their exploitation of it. They naturally had no
cognizance of the physiological background to dreaming, for
they lacked the technical resources to investigate the biochemical processes involved. The physiological function of
the brain was a sealed book to them.

Today dreams are beginning to have significance for us
again, though for other reasons than they did for Indians,
Siberians and Australian aborigines. And this is due to some
new and sensational research data which have recently come
to light.

3

The Nocturnal Cycle

Why do we have to sleep?

The question seems superfluous to anyone who has experienced insomnia, for we know from experience that a good
night's sleep is essential if we are to feel on good form during
the day. But the question of why this is so is less easy to answer.

As recently as the nineteenth century there were widely
differing opinions on the function of sleep, and some fairly
eccentric views were to be heard. The German Sigmund
Exner, for example, suggested that 'the brain cells suspend
their functions during sleep', whatever he meant by that. His
compatriot Hermann Zondeck failed in the attempt to isolate
sleep hormones. The considerably better known French
physiologist Claude Bernard (1813–1878) saw sleep as the
consequence of a reduction in the blood supply to the brain.
And for the great Russian neurophysiologist and Nobel
Prizewinner Ivan Petrovich Pavlov (1849–1936), sleep was
an inhibition of the central nervous system.

We all know what happens when we go to sleep. Often our
eyes begin to itch, the pupils become smaller and the lids
grow heavy. Our heart-beat slows, concentration flags and
our reactions become slower. Our muscles go slack. The

secretion of fluids in the organism, including saliva, stomach fluids and urine, declines sharply. We breathe more slowly and require less air.

The scientific value of the electroencephalogram, which gives a picture of our brain waves, was first discovered by Dr Hans Berger, a neurologist at the University of Jena. To his astonishment, he found that the EEG traced a different pattern for the waking and sleeping states.

In a relaxed waking state with closed eyes, the human brain regularly sends out eight to twelve regular pulses per second and these form what is known as the alpha rhythm. In a light sleep these waves change; they become slower and larger. In deep sleep the EEG registers only one to three pulses per second.

As I have already mentioned, Professor Nathaniel Kleitman of the Department of Physiology at the University of Chicago used Berger's discovery for his sleep research in the 1950s. Night after night he and his assistants – at first Eugene Aserinsky and later William Dement – carried out the first systematic observation of the sleeping state. Kept awake by innumerable cups of coffee, they sat in the ghostly light of the control panels, watching the jagged, spindly lines produced by the EEG and EOG recorders on their rolls of paper.

The recorders produced four basically different brain-wave patterns, indicating that we experience four different depths of sleep. But sleep turned out to be a very different process to that which the scientists had hitherto supposed.

It appeared that during the course of a single night we reach the state of deep sleep more than once.

The scientists discovered to their astonishment that within a seven- to eight-hour period of sleep the progression into and out of deep sleep, through stages 1 to 4, is repeated as many as five times.

The first stage, immediately after we go to sleep, lasts for no more than five minutes. We then pass rapidly through phases

2 and 3 and sink into the fourth phase. This deep sleep lasts for at least half an hour. Then our sleep becomes lighter, and we regain the first phase again in stages. This time the first phase lasts only a few minutes before we once again fall into deep sleep.

In the second nightly cycle of sleep the deep-sleep phase is probably not reached, or if it is, it is for a shorter period than on the first cycle.

One again, the third and second phases give way to the first phase of light sleep, which is followed again by deeper sleep after twenty minutes.

This cycle of sinking into deep sleep and coming out of it again continues throughout the night, each cycle lasting about ninety minutes. As the night goes on we spend longer and longer in the first phase of sleep and phases 3 and 4 become correspondingly shorter. Towards morning we spend most of the time in the first and second phases.

In addition to discovering the cyclic nature of sleep, the American researchers came across another no less startling phenomenon. Analysis of the traces produced by the EOG recorder revealed that the different phases of sleep are associated with particular eye movements.

When we go to sleep and the alpha rhythm fades, our eyes roll gently and slowly, coming to a standstill after a few minutes. The world disappears and bizarre, fragmentary images often appear in its place. Frequently we are jerked out of this early sleep for a fraction of a second by an involuntary convulsion of the muscles. This is caused by a fleeting outburst of activity in the brain.

In the 'sleep laboratory', during this transition into the first phase of sleep, the EEG and EOG recorders trace shallow, irregular curves.

In the first phase we can still be woken easily by a sudden noise and would usually claim that we had not been asleep at all. If left undisturbed we draw progressively further away from the external world and sink into the second phase of sleep. Here the electroencephalogram shows rapid bursts of activity in the form of jagged peaks, and the electro-oculogram traces shallow curves as our eyes move slowly under closed lids. In the third phase, the jagged lines of the EEG recorder change into small, irregular waves, interrupted by large, slow ones. Now blood pressure and body temperature fall, the heart beats more slowly and breathing is slow and regular. Now, unconscious of our surroundings, we reach the fourth phase of sleep. This is characterized by the large regular waves known as delta waves. Some ninety minutes after going to sleep we return from the fourth phase to the third and back into the second phase of light sleep.

At this point Kleitman and his colleagues noted a sudden change. After a subject had returned from phase 2 to phase 1, his eye movements caused a burst of activity on the EOG recorder. The slow eye movements which had been noted hitherto changed suddenly into rapid, violent ones.

In this phase, known as the REM (rapid eye movement) phase, the eyes switch to and fro in unison as if they are watching something. 'It was as if they were watching a game of tennis,' wrote one of the researchers. But that is not all. In this phase the EEG signals a high degree of brain activity and a sleeper displays rising blood pressure, irregular breathing, increased oxygen consumption, a strong heartbeat and, in the case of men, erections. For Kleitman and his colleagues everything seemed to indicate that people in the REM phase of sleep are experiencing strong emotions.

In this paradoxical REM phase of sleep, we are completely detached from the outside world, and it is even more difficult to wake us from it than from phase 4, that of deep sleep.

The Chicago scientists observed to their astonishment that sleepers move restlessly immediately before and after the REM phase. Yet during the course of the REM phase itself they remain absolutely motionless; despite the increased blood pressure, lively brain activity and rapid eye movements, the muscles remain completely relaxed.

As soon as they enter the REM phase, they act exactly like spectators in a theatre, as English psychologist and sleep researcher Ann Faraday described it:

> Before the curtain rises, he shuffles and fidgets in his seat. As the curtain goes up, he becomes still and attentive. The play begins and he follows the action with his eyes: he becomes excited as the plot unfolds, his breathing speeds up, and his heart thumps. As long as the play continues, he is wholly immersed in it, unmoving and unspeaking. When the curtain falls, he moves and stretches, and his former bodily composure is regained. To the early investigators, the analogy seemed almost too good to be true: the sleeper could indeed be watching a play during his periods of REM sleep, but a play of his own making in which he himself was the director, producer, stage manager, principal actor, and audience all at the same time. He must, it seemed obvious, be dreaming.

Kleitman's hypothesis that dreaming occurred during the REM phase, the eye movements indicating that the sleeper was following the dream drama, was the great breakthrough in dream research. A series of experiments was begun in which night after night sleeping subjects were woken by bells during the REM phase and also during the non-REM phase – the period marked by slower eye movements. Over a loudspeaker, they were asked the question: 'Were you dreaming?'

Subjects who were woken out of the REM phase almost always answered sleepily: 'Yes . . . yes I was dreaming.'

'What were you dreaming about?'

'I . . . I was in a corridor . . . in a grey corridor . . . with many doors . . . I was looking for someone . . . I opened a door . . . one door after another, and shouted "Hallo". . . In one room there was a large red telephone on a table. I lifted the receiver and called out: "Hallo, who's there?". . . I heard mocking laughter . . . I felt that I was being observed and looked round. . . A naked woman was standing in the doorway. . . Suddenly the telephone rang loudly, and I woke up.'

The REM phase is repeated as many as five times during a period of sleep, and this means that we are in the dreaming phase for a quarter of the time we are asleep. If it were possible to record all the REM dreams of one man on a film, it would take more than five years to show it.

Sleepers who were woken out of the non-REM phase and asked whether they had been dreaming almost always answered no. Sleep researchers deduced from this that dreaming did not take place during the non-REM phases. But recently it has been proved that this deduction is false. The problem is that everyone thinks of dreams as things that you *see*.

The Concise Oxford Dictionary says that 'to dream' means 'to have visions etc. in sleep'. Usually we remember dreams as a purely visual experience in which we are simultaneously spectator and participant. However, if we define a dream as a series of sensations, thoughts and pictures, or a mixture of all three, the question of whether or not we dream during the non-REM phases of sleep is significantly affected.

Over 10,000 subjects took part in Kleitman's experiments. Of these, 80 per cent answered yes when asked if they had been 'dreaming' when they were woken out of the REM phase, while only 7 per cent of those who were woken out of non-REM phases said they had been 'dreaming'. Because of this, the REM phase was for a long time considered the only one in which dreaming took place. But, of course, the subjects all thought they were being asked about visual dreams.

Later, Dr David Foulkes of the University of Wyoming

conducted a similar series of experiments and came up with very different results, by making a significant alteration in the form of the questions posed to the subjects. Sleepers who were woken out of the non-REM phases, i.e. phases 2, 3 and 4, were no longer asked 'Were you dreaming?' but 'Was anything passing through your mind?' Now, suddenly, 75 per cent of the subjects had been 'dreaming' – something had indeed been passing through their mind, though it was less visual, dramatic or emotional than in the REM phases. Subjects woken out of the REM phase were asked the same question, and the number of those who answered in the affirmative rose to 87 per cent.

Dream expert Ann Faraday says:

Personally, I prefer to use the terms 'REM dream' and 'NREM dream' to distinguish these two kinds of mental activity during sleep. NREM content is often sufficiently dreamlike to make nonsense of the notion that it is either 'non-dreaming' or 'thinking'. And yet it is sufficiently different from REM content that anyone can learn, with a little practice, to distinguish correctly between the two most of the time.

A typical non-REM dream might run as follows:

'I was standing in a garage somewhere and talking to someone about my car . . . I couldn't recognize any of the faces. . . I think I wanted some winter tyres. . . I know I was wondering whether there was still enough anti-freeze in the radiator. . .'

It is interesting that most of the subjects who were woken directly out of both REM and non-REM phases of sleep affirmed that they had been dreaming. But as soon as they were allowed to sleep a whole night through without being woken, they tended to say that they had not been dreaming.

Modern sleep laboratories differ from earlier ones chiefly

through their superior technical facilities. Previously the evaluation of experimental results was a purely visual process. Now this task has been taken over by the computer. The human eye is obviously not capable of detecting the smallest variations in frequency, but the computer is. These variations can be detected by what is known as spectral analysis.

The major breakthrough in this area is mainly due to a research team at the University of California in Los Angeles led by W. R. Adey. The methods used by this team enabled a detailed analysis to be made of the fluctuations in energy experienced by the human brain in both the sleeping and waking states. Aspects of sleep which could not be detected by purely visual analysis of EEG traces can today be distinguished by the computer.

Present-day measuring techniques are so far advanced that they can actually gauge which colour a person is seeing from minute differences in a spectrogram. This is possible because the brain reacts instantly to any sensory stimulus such as smells, changes of light, noise or touch, however fleeting they may be. Likewise, the electroencephalograph registers the minutest traces of these reactions in the brain.

Thus the modern sleep laboratory is, as it were, a seismograph of the soul. Its sophisticated equipment has enabled scientists to throw light on the darkest and most puzzling facet of our existence – the states of sleeping and dreaming which take up a third of our lives.

We now know that everyone dreams throughout his life. Questioning of a representative cross-section of the West German population indicated that every fifth person claims that he never dreams. However, this assumption is based on a misconception. We all dream, even if many of us cannot remember doing so when we wake up.

Experiments carried out as far back as 1957 indicated that so-called 'non-dreamers' do in fact dream. Psychologist

Donald R. Goodenough at the Downstate Medical Center of the State University of New York, together with an intern, Dr Arthur Shapiro, asked sixty student volunteers to state whether they dreamed or not while they were asleep. Those who could remember dreaming practically every night were labelled 'dreamers', while students who claimed to dream very seldom or not at all were classified as 'non-dreamers'. Both groups then had to undergo observation in a sleep laboratory for three nights, eight hours per night. During the course of the experiment, all the students, including the so-called non-dreamers, gave detailed accounts of their dreams.

The fact that we all dream naturally leads to the question of why we have to dream and why we need sleep. Are sleeping and dreaming vital processes, a biological necessity? Or can we exist without sleep or dreams?

This is a question which needs to be answered scientifically. The first scientific experiments in this field were carried out on animals in 1913. Two French researchers, the physiologist Henry Piéron and his assistant Legendre, kept puppies in constant movement for five days on end, not allowing them a moment's sleep. At the end of this period they had reached the limit of their endurance; they were totally exhausted, unable to stand, and simply fell down and went to sleep. All attempts to wake them were in vain; they simply allowed themselves to be dragged around on their leads without waking up.

Since the researchers were investigating the theory that there were sleep centres in the brain which controlled the sleeping process, the dogs were later killed and subjected to a post-mortem examination. The cells of the so-called front brain were found to have undergone a physical change, revealed by discoloration, most notably in the motor region of this part of the brain. From this the experimenters deduced that the sleep centres they were looking for were situated in the front brain. This assumption soon proved to be incorrect,

however. The physical changes discovered were not evidence
of centres controlling the sleeping process, but rather of
damage to those brain cells which had been active during the
long period of sleeplessness.

There are innumerable examples of the devastation which
can be caused by sleep deprivation. Not only today but in
ancient times, the deprivation of sleep was used as a refined
method of torture on particularly hated enemies, which had
the advantage of leaving no trace on the victim. According to
contemporary sources, Perseus (*circa* 212–166 BC) – the last
Macedonian king of the Antigonid dynasty – was deprived of
sleep until he was dead while a captive of the Romans.

Deprivation of sleep is dangerous, and volunteers for sleep
deprivation experiments need not only idealism but a great
deal of courage. During the Second World War over a
hundred volunteers took part in an experiment of this kind at
Camp Elliot in California. The first signs of sleep deprivation
appeared among the soldiers after twenty-four hours. All the
subjects became nervous and irritable. After a further two
days and nights without sleep, many were suffering from
hallucinations. A number of the soldiers who succeeded in
staying awake for a hundred hours paid for it afterwards with
psychoses.

Major Harold Williams, leader of the US Army's department of clinical and social psychology, repeated these experiments in 1956–7 with a research team at the Walter Reed
Army Institute of Research in Washington, D.C. This time
measurements were taken of the effects of sleep deprivation
on psychomotor capability, i.e. the capacity for conscious
coordination and reaction. At a given signal the experimental
subjects had to switch off lights and operate knobs. The
longer they were deprived of sleep, the more unreliable and
irregular were their reactions. These experiments also
demonstrated the serious consequences which sleep deprivation can have. For example, when one of the volunteers was

washing after sixty-five hours of sleep deprivation he suddenly 'saw' spiders' webs hanging from his face, which, in his own
words, he 'vainly tried to wash off'. Another vehemently
refused to drink his milk because he 'saw' hairs floating in it.
Five of the men were convinced they were wearing a hat
which was too small for them. Although naturally none of the
volunteers was wearing any kind of headgear, those affected
repeatedly tried to tear the imaginary hat from their heads.
After ninety hours of sleep deprivation one volunteer doubted
his own identity. He wondered earnestly whether he might
not be someone else, and seemed genuinely unable to
recognize himself. His comrades had to reassure him
repeatedly that he was really still the same person he had
always been.

In 1959 the thirty-two-year-old New York disc jockey
Peter Tripp undertook an almost suicidal marathon wake on
Times Square to raise funds for the Polio Fund of the
National Foundation. He set up his studio in a glass
recruiting kiosk, exposing himself to the gaze of the passers-by
as he became increasingly tired. He managed to go 201 hours
and 13 minutes without sleep.

A suite of rooms in the Astor Hotel across the street had
been turned into a laboratory for the occasion. There a
distinguished and highly paid team of psychiatrists, psychologists and doctors gathered to await results. The direction of the experiment lay in the experienced hands of Dr
Louis Jolyon West – former psychiatrist to the US Air Force
and head of the department of neurology and behavioral
research in the School of Medicine at the University of
Oklahoma – and Major Harold Williams. Peter Tripp was
subjected to a thorough examination beforehand, so that the
scientists would have a picture of his normal functioning to
provide comparative data during the course of the experiment. The disc jockey was under constant medical observation throughout the eight days he succeeded in remaining

awake. His daily programme consisted of his normal daily broadcast and medical, psychological and mental performance tests. In addition EEG recordings were carried out by Columbia University and blood and urine samples were taken. Every two hours Tripp was brought to the laboratory in the Astor Hotel where he was subjected to close examination and was also able to change and take refreshment.

It might be thought that with all this attention and care for his well-being, Tripp would have been fresh and cheerful at least at the beginning of the experiment. But in fact he was soon so tired that he could hardly stand up. No stimulus, whether it was incidents on the street, fresh air, his broadcasts or constant company seemed to make an appreciable difference to his state. After a little more than two days he showed West some spiders' webs which he 'found' as he was changing his shoes. After five days he had to have recourse to stimulants in order not to give up.

Before the experiment began various scientists had warned Tripp of its dangers and alerted him to the phenomena such as hallucinations which it was likely to produce. But none of this had deterred him from his project. The imaginary spiders' webs on his shoes were only the beginning of Tripp's sensory illusions. Next he saw spots on a table-cloth as beetles crawling across it. He also imagined he saw a white poodle leaping around his glass kiosk. This was followed by memory lapses.

After a hundred hours without sleep there was a crisis. Tripp was no longer able to carry out all the tests, and they were reduced to one or two per day. His capacity for concentration was so weakened that the slightest effort seemed to present insuperable problems. The tests became torture not only for Tripp but also for the scientists. One of the psychologists later commented on how frustrating it had been to have to watch a sharp-witted New York disc jockey struggling with the letters of the alphabet.

Tripp's behaviour became increasingly strange and after 110 hours symptoms of delirium set in. He would burst out laughing or take sudden offence for no reason at all. When a doctor in a tweed suit visited him in the kiosk, Tripp saw the pattern on his clothes as 'wriggling worms' which filled him with revulsion. He was also convinced that the two hundred hours set for the experiment had long since passed, but Williams and West lied to him about the time it had already taken in order to keep him going. After about 120 hours, flames 'billowed out' at him when he opened a drawer in the hotel. He ran shrieking out of the building, convinced that the fire had been started deliberately in order to test his reactions. Speaking of this stage in the experiment, West described Tripp as being seriously mentally disturbed.

After 150 hours he had lost his sense of orientation. He didn't know where he was or who he was, and saw 'ghosts'. In his glass kiosk he kept looking distrustfully at a large wall clock, which had changed in his imagination into the heavily made-up face of a well known actor. Finally he began to doubt his own identity and tried to ascertain whether he was not in fact the actor on the wall – i.e. the clock.

The last day of the experiment brought his most harrowing experience of all. A celebrated neurologist had been called in to examine him. But this archaic figure, dressed in a black suit and carrying an umbrella despite the bright sunshine, was too much for Tripp. He willingly obeyed the doctor's request to get undressed and lie naked on the examination table – it was a fad of the neurologist that he would only examine his patients naked. But when Tripp was lying there and saw the man's face peering down at him, he was suddenly seized by the conviction that the doctor was an undertaker, come to bury him alive. He leaped up shrieking and ran out of the room, followed by a team of doctors intent on catching their naked subject. Suspicion and reality had become so confused in Tripp's mind that he finally believed that he was the victim of a conspiracy on the part of the researchers.

After two hundred hours, Peter Tripp, looking pale and hollow-eyed, was brought to the Astor Hotel for a final EEG check. The preparations and testing took an hour and thirteen minutes and then finally he was allowed to sleep.

West predicted that he would fall into 'the deepest sleep in history', and William Dement, who had also witnessed the experiment, was of the opinion that Tripp would fall so deeply alseep that even the REM dream cycle would break down.

The disc jockey slept for thirteen hours and thirteen minutes. When he awoke he felt, in his own words, absolutely fine. The series of tests he was submitted to, indeed, indicated that he was largely his former self again. But the EEG recording of Tripp's brain waves held a big surprise for Dement. It appeared from this that he had not slept particularly deeply or dreamed particularly abundantly. According to the EEG, Tripp had had his first REM dream exactly forty minutes after falling asleep. Of the thirteen hours and thirteen minutes he was asleep, he spent three hours and forty-six minutes in REM phases. Thus 28 per cent of his first sleep for eight days consisted of REM dreams. Normally REM dreams account for approximately 20 per cent of an eight-hour period of sleep, so the figure of 28 per cent is remarkably low. Dement was surprised by this development, and he deduced from it that Tripp was suffering from a substantial suppressed need to dream which would be revealed in additional periods of REM dreaming.

The question of whether Peter Tripp did not in fact dream during the course of his 200 hour wake cannot be answered with certainty. The fact remains that his hallucinations had a strongly dream-like character, which suggests that the brain was trying to make up for the lack of dream phases. In other words, the organism and its psyche seem to look for a means of escape, a way of compensating for the lack of dreams through the medium of hallucinations.

It is also questionable whether in this period of over 200 hours Tripp was in fact totally deprived of sleep. Experiments on sleep deprivation in animals have shown that they are capable of taking 'micro-naps'. The psychologist Wilse B. Webb of the University of Florida at Gainsville, and his assistants, were able to demonstrate this conclusively in their experiments on rats. The animals were put on a moving water wheel in order to prevent them from sleeping. The wheel turned constantly, and as soon as a rat fell asleep he would fall into the cold water below. A few rats showed remarkable endurance, remaining on the wheel for twenty-seven days without stopping. When the scientists analyzed the EEG traces for the period, they found an explanation for this surprising phenomenon: the animals repeatedly went to sleep for second-long periods, and used these micro sleep periods in order to be able to last longer without falling into the water. Finally, however, they were overcome by exhaustion.

It is established, then, that we dream every night and for this reason dreaming cannot effectively be divorced from sleeping. But this naturally leads us to the question: what is more important for us, sleeping or dreaming? We have seen the dramatic effects of sleep deprivation but there have also been experiments on the deprivation of dreams. These were chiefly concerned with the deprivation of REM dreaming because at the time of the experiments it was only this phase which was identified with the phenomenon of dreaming.

The first experiments in so-called dream deprivation were carried out by William Dement, who already had considerable experience in the field of sleep deprivation. His first volunteers were students, employees and an out-of-work actor. None of them were told exactly what the experiment was about and only one condition was made – that they should not sleep during the day. Not even a nap after a meal was allowed.

Dement carried out these first experiments in dream deprivation at Mount Sinai Hospital in New York. He had worked out a method by which the subject was woken by a bell as soon as he entered an REM dream phase, i.e. before the REM dream could take its course. The subjects then had to sit up and were engaged in a short conversation to wake them up completely. Then they were allowed to sleep again, until they were woken once more by the bell. This process was repeated night after night.

It was obviously not possible to achieve a total suppression of REM dreams by this method. The waking process itself – a press on the bell by Dement as soon as the REM phase began and the waking of the subject – lasted a few seconds, during which the REM phase had already begun. It can be compared to what happens when a spectator in the cinema is urgently called to the telephone just as the film begins. Even if he leaves the theatre directly, he will still catch a fragment of the action.

Nevertheless, the subjects who were woken out of REM phases undoubtedly lost 90 per cent of their REM dreams. In the course of the experiment, the scientists came across two interesting facts. First, all those who took part seemed to compensate for the loss of dreaming, for they entered the REM phase more and more frequently. After the fifth night, some of the subjects had to be woken from the REM dream phase as many as twenty or thirty times. After ten days the experiment was abandoned because the participants were then sinking back into REM dreaming immediately after they had been woken. Secondly, in the nights when the subjects were allowed to sleep uninterrupted after the first phase of the experiment, the REM phases increased, often taking up 40 per cent of the whole sleep period. Obviously it was essential for the subjects to catch up on the REM dreams they had missed.

One of Dement's colleagues at Mount Sinai Hospital, the

psychoanalyst Charles Fisher, examined the experimental subjects every day. He discovered that as the nightly experiments progressed they suffered increasingly from lack of concentration, general exhaustion, increased irritability and memory lapses. Muscular coordination was also noticeably affected. Some of the volunteers had already had enough after four nights and only with difficulty could they be persuaded to continue.

During the course of these experiments, a control group was woken, with the same frequency but from the non-REM phases of their sleep. These subjects, unlike the others, showed no apparent ill effects and continued to behave quite normally. From this the scientists concluded that the symptoms produced were caused not by lack of sleep but by lack of dreaming.

A different method of dream deprivation was also tried. Instead of waking the subjects by alarm bells, the researchers gave them drugs – amphetamines for example. With these, the REM phases were successfully suppressed for fifteen nights, but then these experiments too were broken off because noticeable, albeit not serious, personality changes were appearing in the subjects.

It is naturally difficult to judge whether such changes are attributable to dream deprivation or to the drugs themselves, and for this reason experiments of this kind cannot be entirely satisfactory. The symptoms produced in human subjects were one of the main reasons why the researchers returned once more to experiments on animals.

Anyone who has a cat or a dog knows that animals dream. Stretched out on the carpet or in an armchair to sleep the family pet will suddenly move its paws to and fro as if it was running. Its ears twitch, its eyelids flicker, and the animal barks, miaows, grunts or sighs. Obviously it is having an exciting dream – we don't need a sleep researcher to tell us that.

Cats seem to be particularly suited to experiments in sleep deprivation. At any rate it is difficult to deprive a cat of its sleep. Michel Jouvet, Professor of Experimental Medicine at the University of Lyons, has done some particularly valuable research in this field. His experimental cats were obliged to sleep on an upturned tub or a stone in the middle of a pool of water. So long as the animal remained curled up, this did not present any great difficulty. However, as soon as the REM phase began and the muscles relaxed, its head or paws would inevitably slip into the water.

This was a highly convincing way of depriving cats of their dreams, since they hate water. As in the experiments with rats, the cats were also put on a constantly moving water wheel. They had to ride this until overcome by fatigue, at which point they would slip into the water and be woken abruptly from their REM dreams. Like the rats, the cats managed to snatch micro-naps, but they were not enough for the REM phase to appear. In the course of further experiments, the animals were kept in cages and deprived of REM dreams by alarm bells.

Jouvet's main purpose in these experiments was to trace the biochemical substance of which dreams are formed, and in pursuit of this goal some of the unfortunate animals had to wait as long as seventy days before they were allowed to catch up on their REM dreams. Jouvet and his colleagues were convinced that the REM phase of sleep is biochemical in origin. In other words, they assumed that a substance is continuously being produced in the organism – a dream hormone, which is released during REM phases. Spinal fluid was extracted from a cat which had been deprived of dreams for thirty days and injected at the same point into another cat which had not been deprived. As Jouvet and his team had hoped, the REM phases experienced by the second cat increased immediately. According to Jouvet, the severe behavioural disturbances expected after extensive sleep deprivation did not appear. The animals merely behaved a little strangely and their sexual drive showed a disproportionate increase. One tom cat even tried to have intercourse with drugged or dead cats – a completely unnatural pattern of behaviour.

Although Jouvet was unable to prove the existence of a dream hormone, his experiments had another equally sensational result. He succeeded in suspending the blocking of motor activity which normally takes place during the REM phase. This meant that the muscles, instead of being completely slack, as is usually the case during dreaming, were able to function normally. Cats treated in this way would suddenly stand up in the middle of an REM dream and start acting it out. They would spit and scratch at non-existent dogs, lap up non-existent milk from the floor, catch invisible mice and play with them, engage in love-play with imaginary partners. As soon as the REM phase was over, however, they would behave like normal sleeping animals again. Jouvet achieved this effect by surgically removing the underside on the *pons* – a small area at the base of the brain where it joins the spinal cord.

Jouvet also developed a completely new and surprising theory of dreams, suggesting that REM dreams are a means of inculcating behaviour patterns. During the course of his investigations he had discovered that embryos have dreams inside the mother's body. He could even determine how often they dream. He also established that among animals which are fairly self-sufficient after birth, such as calves and foals, the embryo has REM dreams inside its mother's body, but comparatively few after birth. Infant humans, on the other hand, have relatively few REM dreams until shortly before their birth, but as soon as they are born they spend some 80 per cent of their sleep in the REM dream phase. As soon as they become more independent, the REM phases diminish.

A possible explanation of this phenomenon is that in

dreaming we practice particular modes of behaviour in order to be able to carry them out when we are awake. As small children have to practice a great deal, they experience more frequent dream phases than grown-ups. According to this theory, REM dreaming is a training session for instinctive behaviour.

The theory is supported by experiments carried out by the American researcher Dr Johann Stoyva and his colleagues at the University of Colorado. Stoyva made his subjects wear special spectacles which turned the world upside down, and while his experimental group were getting accustomed to this upside-down world they had appreciably more REM dreams than usual.

The answers to the question of why we need to sleep and dream seem endless. It has also been proved that in the non-REM phases, particularly phases 3 and 4, growth hormones are released. These hormones are used for the maintenance and growth of the body and in addition they are absolutely indispensable for protein synthesis. Significantly, adolescents spend an exceptional amount of time in the non-REM phases of sleep – a scientific proof of the old adage that sleep before midnight is the most valuable for children and adolescents.

The necessity of the REM phases of sleep is proved both by Jouvet's theory and also by another according to which REM dreams produce an important protein in the brain. This protein is needed by the brain cells for their functioning and development.

Dreaming would also seem to have another important function, assisting in the complex biochemical processes of memory and helping with the processing and storage of new information. If we compare the brain with a computer, the dreaming carries out the essential task of programming. Learning and remembering both have close links with dreaming. But no one, including the biochemist, would claim that this is the whole story. These physiological processes do not explain, for example, why we often dream that we are flying, or falling into an abyss. Clearly the physiological approach alone is not sufficient to explain the seemingly irrational world of dreams, that second reality. The meaning of dreams has traditionally been the province of the psychologist and particularly the psychoanalyst. But is the traditional interpretation of dreams still valid in a contemporary context?

4

Anatomy of an Island

I seemed to be standing on high ground—the upper slopes of some spur of a hill or mountain. The ground was of a curious white formation. Here and there in this were little fissures, and from these jets of vapour were spouting upward. In my dream I recognized the place as an island of which I had dreamed before—an island which was in imminent peril from a volcano. And, when I saw the vapour spouting from the ground, I gasped: 'It's the island! Good Lord, the whole thing is going to *blow up*!' For I had memories of reading about Krakatoa, where the sea, making its way into the heart of a volcano through a submarine crevice, flashed into steam, and blew the whole mountain to pieces. Forthwith I was seized with a frantic desire to save the four thousand (I knew the number) unsuspecting inhabitants. Obviously there was only one way of doing this, and that was to take them off in ships. There followed a most distressing nightmare, in which I was at a neighbouring island, trying to get the incredulous *French* authorities to despatch vessels of every and any description to remove the inhabitants of the threatened island. I was sent from one official to another; and finally woke myself by my own dream exertions, clinging to the heads of a team of horses drawing the carriage of one 'Monsieur le Maire', who was going out to dine and wanted me to return when his office would be open next day. All through the dream the *number* of the people in danger obsessed my mind. I repeated it to everyone I met, and, at the moment of waking, I was shouting to the 'Maire', 'Listen! Four thousand people will be killed unless . . .'

This account is given by the English mathematician Professor J. W. Dunne in his controversial book *An Experiment with Time*, which was published in 1927. Even today, the book has the same startling impact as it had when it first came out.

In the spring of 1902, Dunne was with the 6th Mounted Infantry encamped near the ruins of Lindley in what was then the Boer Republic of the Orange Free State. 'We had just come off *trek*,' wrote Dunne, 'and mails and newspapers arrived but rarely. There, one night, I had an unusually vivid and rather unpleasant dream.'

'This dream is not so easy to interpret,' says the great Greek doctor and philosopher Hippocrates to his professional peers Sigmund Freud and Carl Gustav Jung – his juniors by some 2300 years. (We may imagine them perched on a cloud in some latter-day Olympus.) 'As you must know from your history books, I come from an ancient family of priests on the island of Kos in the Aegean Sea. I lived between 460 and 375 BC. Secret knowledge of the art of healing was traditionally handed down from father to son in my family. This magical medicine, which your colleagues so often scorn today, originated with the Babylonians and Egyptians, and was preserved in temple records.

'In my time these now ruined temples were consecrated to Aesculapius, the god of healing. In fact, amazingly enough, the staff of the god Aesculapius with a snake entwined round it is still used as a symbol of the medical profession today, though a great deal else about it has changed. However that may be, the most famous of the temples of Aesculapius stood on Kos and at Epidaurus, Athens, Pergamum and Rome, and sick people came to visit them in order to learn the prescription for their cure. This information was revealed to them during sleep in deliberately induced dreams.

'You, gentlemen, may find it incomprehensible that in those days we saw a close relationship between the state of the body and the positions of the stars. But according to current belief, the whole universe and every cosmic event had a symbolic significance for a man's state of health. And it is largely due to me that this vision of the world was rationalized and incorporated into a system.

'For me, then, it is entirely natural to see a brightly shining star in a dream as a sign of good health. Nor should you forget, gentlemen, that in my time the universe was peopled with gods and every cosmic happening was personified in some form or other. For me, the sun, moon and stars are an effective psychic expression of an organic and biological state.

'A sick man who came to my temple – my clinic as you would call it – was exposed to a strongly suggestive atmosphere, which contributed to the healing process. Everything was designed to favour the patient's recuperation. It began with the religious rites performed in honour of Aesculapius, with cold baths, special diets, the prohibition of alcohol, sacrifices, and other measures. The sick besought the gods to send them healing dreams in meditation and prayer. Then they lay down to sleep amid the beautiful surroundings of the temple, lulled by music and overlooked by exquisite statues. The temple servants extinguished the torches and a large yellow snake which was consecrated to the god of healing moved silently among the dreamers.

'Obviously there is no comparison with the clinics of your own time. You, my dear Jung, as a psychologist, will understand that these are the ideal conditions for healing. They make it possible for a soul, in particular, to aid the process of convalescence.'

Jung nods comprehendingly, but Freud is not so sure. 'What do you mean by that?' he asks.

'It's quite simple,' says Hippocrates with a smile. 'We know from experience that in the waking state the soul is fully occupied with the body's functioning – seeing, thinking, hearing, feeling. Only in sleep – in dreaming – is the soul free to devote all its strength to the body's state of health.'

'Does he mean that it can devote itself to suppressed desires?' Freud asks Jung.

'Typical,' says Jung to Hippocrates. 'He can't leave them alone even here.'

'In any case,' Hippocrates continues, 'all the successful cures at that time were inscribed on the temple walls, together with the diagnosis of the illness and the divine prescription revealed in the patient's dreams. Over the course of the centuries a whole library of dream cures was collected in this way, whose effectiveness had been proved by experience.

'But let us return to Dunne's dream. I find it difficult to interpret, since I do not know whether he saw stars in the sky when he was dreaming. For stars which are in the wrong position or look cloudy are a sure indication of physical illness. If they do not appear in a dream at all, we can expect the illness to be fatal.

'In Dunne's case, I would say on the basis of our experience that he is about to suffer a severe illness. The symbolism of the erupting volcano is in itself an indication of this. Did you know, gentlemen, that dreams about overflowing rivers or rising vapours, for instance, indicate high blood pressure and fever, while springs signify diseases of the bladder and withered branches mean impotence?'

'I can certainly see a withered branch indicating fear of impotence,' Freud agrees.

'For me, Mr Dunne's dream symbolizes high blood pressure and an attack of fever,' continues Hippocrates impatiently. 'It's equally obvious that it must be a contagious illness. The island with its threatened population is a symbol of this. But the most interesting aspect of this dream in my opinion is the fact that the dreamer is seeking help for his illness. This is obvious from the fact that he approaches "Monsieur le Maire" and asks him to help the threatened population. At the same time the dreamer knows instinctively that this help will be denied him. Finally the figure 4000 is significant. The number four symbolizes Dionysus, the god of fertility and wine. This could be an indication that the illness is to be treated with poultices using wine.

'At any rate, if Mr Dunne had lived in my time, I would have invited him to come to my clinic on Samos for treatment.'

'With all due respect to my colleague's impeccable reputation, I feel obliged to veto his suggestions.' The interruption comes from Sigmund Freud, neurologist and founder of modern psychoanalysis. 'I'm afraid I cannot share your view that Dunne would be likely to fall ill through the influence of the stars in his dream. Naturally I fully understand that diagnostic methods in your day were very different from those used in mine, but times have changed and so have people's attitudes. I must remind you that I lived between 1856 and 1939 and was able to profit from research methods which had not even been dreamed of in your time.

'For me, dreaming is primarily a psychic phenomenon. Its interpretation is the royal road to knowledge of the subconscious, and hence the surest basis for psychoanalysis. Before I analyse Mr Dunne's dream, I would like to explain briefly how I came to understand this.

'Right at the beginning of my career, I observed that a series of my patients complained of headaches, impaired vision, paralysis and similar ills which had no apparent physical cause. Psychically, they often suffered from anxiety states, fixed ideas and similar disorders. This led me to the conclusion that all these sufferings could have an emotional cause. I soon discovered that these symptoms of illness disappeared when my patients could talk to me freely about their problems. This was particularly often the case when they suddenly remembered unpleasant aspects of their affective life which they had forgotten. These were mostly sexual impulses and aggressive behaviour which had their origins in childhood. I concluded that the painful or shameful memory of these desires and actions had led to their suppression. In my view they then reappeared in the guise of symptoms of illness.'

'Just a minute,' interposes Hippocrates. 'You're lecturing us about suppressed sexual impulses which have led to severe illness in your patients. I feel sure this must be a contemporary phenomenon, a feature of your own century. As far as I can remember, love as we used to call it was not generally suppressed in my time. But what has all this got to do with dreams?'

'Well, I observed that my patients spoke most freely when they were lying on a couch,' answers Freud. 'This technique, known as free association, would occasionally bring to mind a dream which a patient had had, which released a chain of thoughts and memories. Many of these dreams, however, were in themselves an indication of suppressed needs and desires, and consequently responsible for neurotic symptoms. This led me to the idea of analysing both my own dreams and those of my patients. I slowly became convinced that suppressed desires need some kind of surrogate fulfilment which takes the form of symptoms of illness in the waking state and dreams during sleep.'

'Dreams as wish-fulfilment? What ever makes you think that?' asks Hippocrates in astonishment.

'Tell him,' says Jung encouragingly.

'Nothing but the study of my own dreams,' says Freud.

'On the one hand the dream experiences we have every night resemble mental illnesses both inwardly and outwardly, but on the other hand they are comparable with an entirely healthy waking existence. In our waking state we treat dreams just as the patient does his psychoanalyst. Both are usually quickly and completely forgotten. We don't pay much attention to our dreams because they are mostly of such a doubtful character. And even when they are not confused or senseless, we don't change our opinion of them, because our other dreams are such obvious nonsense. We banish them from our memory because of the shamelessness and "immorality" which are evident in many of our dreams.'

'That's an absurdly pessimistic view of the matter,' says Hippocrates. 'No one in my own age would dream of sharing it with you.'

'That may well be,' pursues Freud. 'On the other hand I can tell you that many people in my society share your contemporaries' view that dreams are a glimpse of the future, even if they are inclined to doubt the value of dreaming. But I don't think one need substitute mystical ideas for lack of knowledge. I never succeeded myself in discovering any proof of the prophetic nature of dreams.

'For the dreamer, all dreams are confused, incomprehensible and strange. But if one looks at the dreams of very small children, say about eighteen months old, one will find them remarkably simple and easy to understand. Small children dream of the fulfilment of wishes which have been frustrated during the preceding day. One doesn't need any great skill in interpretation to deduce this – one need only ask a child about his experiences during the previous day – the dream day. Now it would simplify our task greatly if the dreams of adults could be unravelled as easily as those of children – if in fact they were the fulfilment of wishes and impulses which had occurred during the dream day. And this is in fact the case. Moreover the analysis of dreams shows clearly how the subconscious makes use of particular symbols – especially in connection with sexual problems. This symbolism may vary from one individual to another, but it is at least partly characteristic, and seems to tie in with the symbols on which our myths and legends are based. Their presence in popular verbal traditions may well be explained by their appearance in dreams.

'But to turn to Dunne's dream, I would first of all like to say that it is impossible to interpret a dream without having access to the unconscious thoughts which lie behind the content of a dream. In the case of my patients, these are revealed to me through the technique of free association. In view of the unusual circumstances – and the distinguished company in which we find ourselves – I will certainly hazard an interpretation, but I can't be responsible for its accuracy.

'For me this dream contains one important clue. This is the fact that Dunne starts by dreaming of the place – the island – which he has already seen before. This particular locality about which he has a sense of *déjà vu* always has a particular significance in dreams, representing the genitals of the mother. Even the significant word fissures is mentioned in connection with it. The dream clearly shows Dunne's subconscious childhood wish to have sexual intercourse with his mother. But the words "Good Lord, the whole thing is going to blow up!" hint at the anxiety and danger connected with this wish. It is a demonstration of the typical Oedipus complex.'

'I saw my old friend Sophocles's tragedy, *Oedipus*, in Athens,' observes Hippocrates, 'but I can't for the life of me remember that Oedipus had a complex in it.'

'You would probably never have dreamed either that your contemporary's King Oedipus would become the cornerstone of my psychoanalysis over two thousand years later,' replies Freud maliciously, 'but to make things a little clearer, I'll just refresh our memories about the Oedipus legend.

'The king of Thebes, Menelaus, and his wife Jocasta, had a

son whose name was Oedipus. He was exposed on a mountainside as an infant, because his father had learned from the oracle that his as yet unborn son would later be his murderer. But Oedipus was saved and brought up in a foreign court. Unaware of his origins, he one day visited the oracle himself and was advised to avoid his homeland, since he would otherwise slay his father and marry his mother. He left what he supposed to be his homeland, but on the way met King Menelaus, whom he slew in a sudden quarrel. Outside the gates of the city of Thebes, he solved the riddle of the Sphinx, who was blocking the way, and was elected king by the Thebans in gratitude. At the same time he was married to Jocasta, unaware that she was his own mother. He lived peacefully for many years and his mother bore him two sons and two daughters, but then a plague broke out. The Thebans asked the oracle for advice, and learned that the plague would cease once the murderer of Menelaus had been driven from the land.

'The dream of having intercourse with one's mother – of taking the father's place, in other words – is one still shared by many men today, as it was then. It is a feeling which surprises and shocks them. This suppressed desire and the youth's feelings of rivalry with his father are the cause of the so-called Oedipus complex.

'In Dunne's dream Monsieur le Maire is the father figure. Dunne clings to the heads of the horses, and the animals themselves represent the sexual drive – the libido – which he envies the father in his relations with the mother. Finally the destructive aspects of the dream reveal the subconscious death-wish which is common to all men.'

'But this is where the whole weakness of your theory lies, my dear Freud.' The Swiss psychologist and psychiatrist Carl Gustav Jung (1875–1961) turns to his former teacher. 'In my view you only see causes in Dunne's dream, without enquiring into the reason.

'What is the reason for this dream? That is the fundamental question, and one which you have not answered. I don't believe that the dream contains an element of wish-fulfilment. Your school operates with purely bodily sex symbols, but in reality your concept of sexuality is so flexible and vague that it can be applied to practically anything. You insist on the view that the sexual instinct rules everything. In your opinion the sexual drive is always dominant, in the sick man and the healthy, and in dreaming as well.

'For me the dream experience is of a far more profound nature. I believe that the most important elements in dreaming have their origin not in the sexual but the religious sphere. This is why I also believe that there is an element of the unknown in dream symbolism which is not only hard to recognize, but defies exact definition. Let us take the so-called phallic symbols, for example. According to your analysis they are a direct representation of the male member. But from a purely psychological point of view the penis is already a symbol in itself, whose deeper meaning is not so easy to define. As you will know from your own experience, my dear Hippocrates, the use of phallic symbols was common in the ancient world, but no one thought of confusing the phallus as a ritual symbol with the penis. Even today, primitive peoples still use this symbolism. The phallus has always been regarded as a source of creative energy – the force of healing and fertility, a force of unlimited strength.

'In mythology and dreams this force is symbolized by the bull, the donkey, the pomegranate, the goat, lightning, the horse's hoof, dancing, the process of menstruation, and many others. These archaic symbols – which we can call archetypes – are perpetuated in myths and dreams and express subconscious thoughts which are common to the whole human race. They appear in our dreams, conquering the limitations of space and time. The whole mythology and racial experience of man is enshrined in this collective

unconscious. Our human instincts are a valuable storehouse
of images from the depths of time, which help to determine
the fate of every one of us.

   'For you, Freud, there is only a single archetype: incest – the Oedipus motif. For you the libido is a purely sexual
force, whereas I see it as a source of some far less definable
form of psychic energy. You treat the unconscious mind as a
reservoir of infantile impulses and suppressed drives. I regard
it as a means of access to the collective unconscious of all
mankind, a channel to the source of a profound wisdom.

   'However one may interpret Dunne's dream, that interpretation only has a meaning if it satisfies Dunne himself. For
you the meaning of the dream seems obvious. For me it is far
less clear, but I think I can make a few comments on it. I
believe that this dream has its origins in the collective
unconscious, for I recognize some archetypal symbols: the
island, the heat, the vapours, the ships, Monsieur le Maire
and the horses.

   'The dream is an eruption, a breaking out and a reaching
towards spiritual freedom in the search for God. The island,
the vapours and the heat represent the soul. The explosion
and the ships represent the eruption and flight, while the
father figure of Monsieur le Maire embodies the divine being.
For me the horses do not represent the sexual drive, as they do
for you, but a psychic force striving for fulfilment.'

Let us leave Hippocrates, Freud and Jung, and turn to
Dunne himself. Would he be satisfied with the interpretations given, or at least with one of them?

   Most important, what does he say about his dream himself?
In fact he wrote:

   I am not certain now when we received our next batch
   of papers, but, when they did come, the *Daily Telegraph*

was amongst them, and, on opening the centre sheet, this is what met my eyes:

VOLCANO DISASTER
IN
MARTINIQUE

TOWN SWEPT AWAY

An Avalanche of Flame

PROBABLE LOSS OF OVER
40,000 LIVES

British Steamer Burnt

One of the most terrible disasters in the annals of the world has befallen the once prosperous town of St Pierre, the commercial capital of the French island of Martinique in the West Indies. At eight o'clock on Thursday morning the volcano Mont Pelée which had been quiescent for a century. . .

But there is no need to go over the story of the worst eruption in modern history.

In another column of the same paper was the following, the headlines being somewhat smaller:

A MOUNTAIN EXPLODES

There followed the report of the schooner *Ocean Traveller,* which had been obliged to leave St Vincent owing to a fall of sand from the volcano there, and had subsequently been unable to reach St Lucia owing to adverse currents opposite the ill-fated St Pierre. The paragraph contained these words: 'When she was about a mile off, the volcano Mont Pelée exploded.'

The narrator subsequently described how the mountain seemed to split open all down the side.

Needless to say, ships were busy for some time after, removing survivors to neighbouring islands.

At first the mathematician in Dunne refused to accept the possibility that his dream had been a premonition of the volcanic eruption. Had he perhaps read the article about the eruption and simultaneously thought that he had already dreamed about it? Dunne rejected this notion, and the idea of a telepathic transference through the journalist who had written the article, after carrying out a research project based on dreams of this nature.

In this project, Dunne noted and analysed every detail of the dreams of experimental subjects over a number of years. He finally came to the conclusion that practically everyone has dreams in which they experience future events. Mostly these events are so trivial that people seldom remember that they have dreamed them when they actually happen. Usually it is only the most drastic events – like the volcanic eruption – which we are able to associate with a previous dream experience.

Dunne did not see the phenomenon of prophetic dreaming as some occult or extrasensory process. He was after all a mathematician. In his view the experience of a linear succession of events in our world of past, present and future was nothing but an illusion.

According to J. W. Dunne time has more than one dimension and this is why we often dream of the future. Thus while an event can be in the past in one dimension, it may be in the future in another. In other words, events may appear in particular dreams which have already happened in one dimension, but are yet to come in another dimension.

At the beginning of his account, Dunne mentioned that he was reminded in his dream of the volcanic eruption of Krakatoa, which he had read about. One wonders if he also knew what had happened in connection with this catastrophe.

On 28 August 1883 the *Boston Globe* published a front-page story about a gigantic volcanic eruption. A young journalist named Byron Somes described in horrific detail the explosion of an island in the Indonesian archipelago. Details of this dreadful catastrophe took weeks and months to reach America because of the long sea voyage involved, but fortunately for the young reporter they confirmed his account in every detail, for his story had practically cost him his job. It now appeared that the volcano had first erupted on 26 August, but it was not until 28 August, when Somes's report had already appeared in the Boston newspaper, that the volcano finished its deadly work and the island of Krakatoa sank into the sea.

5

Temples of Dreams

In many cultural traditions dreams appear repeatedly as a foretaste of future events. We all know the Pharaoh's dream of the seven fat and seven lean cows, which Joseph interpreted as meaning seven fruitful years to be followed by seven years of famine. And most of us probably remember the dream of Calpurnia, the third wife of Julius Caesar, who dreamed of his murder the night before his death and besought him in vain not to go to the Senate. Thus dreams not only reach into the past, but also show images from the future.

People often deny the prophetic nature of dreams on the grounds that they imply a predetermined future, allowing no room for free will or choice.

For the great cultures of the past, the question of free will or choice did not exist. There was no point in worrying about such matters in a universe inhabited by gods who ruled the elements and guided the fate of men. Mankind was at the mercy of the vagaries of destiny. But through their dreams the Babylonians, Egyptians or Greeks could at least receive some indication, some prior warning, of what was in front of them.

In those days, as today, men had recourse to an interpreter

in order to learn the 'true meaning' of their dreams. In our age, this function is assumed by the psychiatrist, but in those days there were professional dream interpreters, who were highly respected and lived in temples. In ancient Egypt, these temples, dedicated to Serapis, the god of dreams, were distributed throughout the country. One of the most important temple complexes of the period was the Serapeum in Memphis, built around 3000 BC. The interpreters who lived in the temples were known as the 'wise men of the magic library'; a sign was found over the entrance to one of the rooms in which they officiated with the inscription: 'By the might of the god, I interpret dreams. Good luck. The dream interpreter here is called Cretan.'

Throughout the ancient world it was the custom to spend the night in these temples, in the hope of inducing dreams. The practice was known as incubation. Prayer and fasting were also employed towards the same end. Occasionally, someone who did not have the time to spare would send another man as his representative. If all else failed, the Egyptians had recourse to magical rites in order to induce dreams. They would write the name of five gods on a clean linen bag, then fold this tightly together and twist it into a lamp wick. This would be soaked in oil and set alight. Before the supplicant went to sleep, he would go up to the lamp and conjure it by means of a magic formula seven times in succession. Then he would extinguish the flame and lie down to sleep, in the hope that his questions would be answered in a dream.

One of the most dramatic dreams of all time, and one which influenced a whole nation, is engraved on a reddish granite tablet between the paws of the great Sphinx of Giza. This great stone figure, 60 feet high, has the body of a lion and the head of a man, which probably represents the ancient Egyptian ruler Khaphre. However, it was also worshipped as an image of the god Harmadis (= Horus, the king of gods).

According to tradition, the Egyptian Thutmose once lay down in the shadow of the Sphinx and went to sleep. The god appeared to him in a dream and ordered him to save his temple from ruin by removing the quicksand into which it was in danger of sinking. If he did this, the god promised, he would be rewarded with the crown of Egypt.

The account of the dream of Thutmose which has lain between the paws of the Sphinx for more than three thousand years, runs as follows:

It happened that when Thutmose on his mid-day walk, lay down in the shadow of the great god to rest, he was overcome by sleep. When the sun stood exactly at the zenith, he had a dream, and it seemed to him as if the god opened his mouth and spoke to him:

'Contemplate me, look at me, my son Thutmose. I am your father. The kingdom shall be yours . . . the earth in its length and breadth belong to you . . . plenty and riches shall be yours. You will be granted many years of life . . . the best of all things shall belong to you. . .

'The sand of the region in which I pass my existence has covered me up. Promise me to fulfil my heart's desire; then I will acknowledge you as my son and helper.'

When he later became pharaoh of Egypt, Thutmose IV (late fifteenth century BC) carried out the duty he had been pledged to fulfil in his dream. He regarded it as his main task to preserve the temple of the god – the Sphinx of Giza – and have it excavated from the quicksand by his subjects.

The importance attached to dreams in ancient Egypt is demonstrated by the Chester Beatty papyrus. In this document, over 200 dreams and their interpretations are recorded by the priest of the god Horus. The dreams are chiefly about games and drinks, correct behaviour, bestiality, incest and female sexual behaviour. A typical example runs as follows:

If a married woman dreams that she kisses her husband, she will have difficulties.

If she couples with a horse in her dream, she will be violent towards her husband.

If on the other hand she couples with a donkey, she will have to atone for her stupidity.

But if she has intercourse with a ram, she will gain the favour of the pharaoh.

If a wether couples with her, she will fall dead on the spot.

If she sleeps with a Syrian, tears are in store for her, because she has had intercourse with a slave.

If she gives birth to a cat, she will have many children.

If she brings a dog into the world, she will bear a son.

If she brings a donkey into the world, she will give birth to an idiot.

Lists of 'do's and don't's' are frequently given, e.g.:

Eating crocodile flesh – good: he will become an official.
Looking into a deep well – bad: imprisonment lies ahead.
Sexual intercourse by daylight – bad: his god sees his misdeeds.

The reasons for the classification of something as good or bad are not given.

Unlike the Babylonians, the Egyptians had little belief in demons. They accepted their dreams rather as messages from the gods. These gods were considered to have three functions in the dreams: they demanded penances, warned the dreamer of imminent danger and answered his questions.

Despite the varying attitudes towards dreams at different times and in different places, they played an important part in shaping the life of the ancient world. Everyone went to the dream temples – military leaders and statesmen as well as the ordinary people – to learn from the gods how they should carry out their tasks and what would be the result of their actions.

Thus the interpretation of dreams was an important task, and good interpreters were highly paid men. A dream encyclopedia written by the Greek Artemidorus of Ephesus at the beginning of the second century AD caused a sensation. It is reputed that Artemidorus, the first Greek to deal with the theory of dreams, once said: 'I have done nothing but think day and night about the evaluation and interpretation of dreams.'

He journeyed extensively, visiting incubation temples, talking to dream interpreters and buying up manuscripts on the subject. Among the latter were a number of dream books which had once been part of the Babylonian library of king Assurbanipal (669–626 BC) at Nineveh. Artemidorus saw visions of future events in many of the dreams he studied, and was of the opinion that they were given to men so that they might learn something and benefit from them. He held the view that an interpreter must know all the details of a dream before he can interpret it. When the beginning of a dream is unclear, he claimed, it is best to start with the end and investigate the source later. When different people had the same dream, one should not assume that they had the same meaning, in fact it was absolutely essential to obtain detailed information about each dreamer and his circumstances before the dream was interpreted.

Despite this doctrine of individual interpretation, Artemidorus left long lists of dreams in his books, which were arranged in categories according to their content. For example, it was a good omen for a farmer if he dreamed of ants, as they are industrious and represent fertility. To dream of a tapeworm meant that an enemy was sitting at the table. To dream that one was dead, however, was a wonderful omen for fathers, poets, writers, orators and philosophers. It meant that the father would see his children grow up strong, handsome and intelligent, while the others would produce works which would be greeted with acclaim.

In the course of time, innumerable dream interpreters copied, plagiarized and adapted Artemidorus's original work. It became the ancestor of all books on dream interpretation and its influence remains surprisingly strong even today. In a book of interpretations published in 1976 the dreams are arranged in alphabetical order, as follows:

Ape means sickness and infirmity.

Cow brings profit, depending on the number of calves.

Flame brings a quarrel with a loved one, which ends well.

Mule means illness.

Onion means a valuable treasure will be discovered if it is eaten (in the dream of course).

Ploughing means for a young woman who sees a man ploughing, a serious, hard-working husband.

She-goat means happiness during the coming weeks.

Virgin brings a man intense pleasure (not always).

Yoke represents imminent marriage.

Zulu (black man) means a danger to health, happiness in love disturbed.

And this was in the year 1976, in the age of computers and space travel! In *The Science of Dreams* the contemporary American author Edwin Diamond wrote: 'In one regard the successors seemed to be superior to the master. Their choice of titles showed greater imagination than anything Artemidorus might have conjured up.'

An English dream book of the eighteenth century, for example, bears the title: 'Dreams and Moles with their Interpretation and Signification made far more Manifest and Plain than any Published to the very meanest Capacities, by the most ancient as well as the most modern Rules of Philosophy.'

But there is one thing which all the dream books of past ages have in common: a belief in the prophetic significance of many dreams. From time immemorial, men have believed that dream experiences represent another level of reality and provide a foretaste of the future. Many of us still share this belief – or is it superstition? – today.

Scientists may calmly condemn it as superstition. But man is a superstitious animal, whether he likes it or not, and even scientists are not immune in this respect. Some of them would class as superstition everything which cannot be reconciled with modern scientific knowledge. Others think of superstition rather as a belief in the perception and operation of forces which cannot be explained by natural laws. This attitude, however, is a proof of superstition in itself, for electricity, electromagnetic forces and gravity are all forces which cannot be explained satisfactorily, yet science still believes in them.

Today the life of every inhabitant of the earth is influenced by ideological, religious or scientific 'superstitions'. We may smile at superstition, but it rules the world.

If then we are not prepared to dismiss the so-called prophetic nature of dreams out of hand as occult nonsense – and it is worth remembering that there are a substantial number of scientists who are not – how is it to be explained?

One possible answer is J. W. Dunne's theory that time has several dimensions. Another is that future events are predetermined, only awaiting a cause to set them in motion.

Just as dreams are rooted deep in the past, so may they also lead from past to future events, for the subconscious instinctively grasps which future event must necessarily follow a past one.

In a number of Indian states, including Madras, are preserved what must surely be the most mysterious libraries in the world. These are ancient collections of palm-leaf manuscript. Carefully arranged bundles of palm leaves some 35 mm wide have been used for centuries to record the lives of men living today. Practically anyone who presents himself in person can pay a few rupees to have his palm leaf brought out and read to him. The two sides of the leaf contain twenty-three and twenty-six lines written in an ancient Tamil verse form. The characters are only about a millimetre high, and scarcely legible to the naked and unpractised eye. The inscription includes not only the name of the visitor but also those of his parents, the number and names of his brothers and sisters, his children, his exact trade or profession and even physical peculiarities.

The most amazing part of this phenomenon seems to be that the palm leaf always bears the exact name of the person in question, and only includes those relatives who are still alive on the day when he pays his visit. The past life of the visitor is related in picturesque detail, as if the writer of the inscription had taken part in it personally, though he is of course long since dead. Details of the future are also included – unmarried enquirers may learn the name and other details of their future partner. Often the inscription even includes the date on which the enquirer will visit the palm-leaf library, and the name of the person who introduces him to it.

Two palm leaves are set out for each visitor. The first one bears his name and profession and an account of his former life. If all the details given correspond with the facts, then the second palm leaf is read out. However, this can only take place on a day which is named on the first leaf. It is from the second leaf that the enquirer learns about his future. Future events up to his death are grouped in sections of two and a half to five years.

The content of the inscriptions on the palm leaves is said to have been drawn from two different sources – firstly from highly detailed astrological calculations, and secondly from the clairvoyant capacities of the Indian sages of ancient times.

Many people will naturally wonder how it is possible to preserve the life stories of thousands of millions of men on a mere pile of palm leaves, but in fact the question does not arise, for the palm leaves are prepared and preserved only for those who will visit a library and ask for their individual leaf. Even this, of course, is no simple task.

It is claimed that the sages who recorded all these details on the palm leaves centuries ago also calculated and foresaw who would one day come to visit the libraries. Now according to the modern scientific way of thinking, it is totally impossible for a man to know the name and life story of another man centuries before his birth. In the Indian tradition, however, this type of prophecy is known as 'Brighu Santa', owing its origin to a sage by the name of Brighu. It is said that Brighu's interest in prophesy was prompted by concern for the fate of his pupils, and that he finally discovered this way after many years of meditation.

Occasionally pictorial explanations are given on the palm leaves of words and concepts which did not exist centuries ago. These have to be interpreted; for example the occupation of engine driver is described as follows: 'He who guides a contrivance which carries many men over long distances with the help of steam.'

One of the highest ranking judges in India caused considerable embarrassment to the owner of a palm-leaf collection which had been in his family for many generations. The archivist had begun reading the judge his palm leaf, which corresponded to the facts in every detail. Suddenly the man refused to read any further and, pretending that something was wrong, got up to fetch another palm leaf. The judge, however, would not let him go, and forced him to read on – having a fair idea of what was coming. Trembling with fear, the owner of the palm leaves told the judge that he had committed adultery with his own mother-in-law. He was right.

One of the many people to visit a palm-leaf library was the Buddhist monk and traveller Lama Anagarika Govinda, the author of *The Way of the White Clouds*. Govinda, who is in fact an Englishman, confirmed that all the information given on the palm leaf corresponded exactly with the details of his own life.

According to Tamil tradition, the palm-leaf inscriptions are closely linked with the phenomenon of dreaming. They are, in fact, nothing more than prophetic dreams of a person's life.

Every cultural tradition contains accounts of the life and works of seers who were able to foretell the future, but to find genuine cases of people gifted with prophetic powers is like looking for a needle in a haystack. Naturally there must be strong enough proof to dispose of the possibility of mere coincidence. On the other hand, if we say that the past is dead and the future not yet born, we confine ourselves to a life on the borders of two inaccessible planes of existence, and this is both scientifically and philosophically untenable.

Let us assume that the past and future are no less real than the present, that they are merely stages in changes taking place in the universe before and after a certain arbitrary point called now. In this case it is possible to see past events or even glimpse future possibilities.

Thus wrote the Australian writer Andrew Tomas, who was born in St Petersburg in 1913.

There are occurrences which seem to support this view, however paradoxical it may appear. And if we subscribe to it, our customary view of time loses its validity and we find ourselves faced once more with the question of what constitutes reality, of the possible dimensions of our existence.

6

Time-Shift

In August 1901 two Englishwomen visited Paris. They were Annie Moberley, Principal of St Hugh's College in Oxford and a colleague, Dr Eleanor Frances Jourdain. After a short stay in the capital they went on to Versailles. Later, after returning to England, they published a report on their journey which describes what must be some of the most remarkable events of our century.

The two Englishwomen visited the palace at Versailles, where after touring the building itself they descended the steps into the gardens, walking towards the Petit Trianon. There they turned off along a track and passed by some deserted farm buildings, in front of which there was an old plough. On the path stood two men in long green coats, wearing three-cornered hats. Eleanor Jourdain asked them the way and they replied with dignified gestures, from which the two Englishwomen gathered that they should go straight on. They went on their way, without giving another thought to the strangers' period costume, assuming it to be intended as a tourist attraction. They strolled up to an isolated cottage, where a woman and a twelve- or thirteen-year-old girl were standing at the doorway, both wearing white kerchiefs fastened under their bodices. As Eleanor Jourdain described the scene, the woman was standing at the top of the steps, holding a jug and leaning slightly forwards, while the girl stood beneath her, looking up at her and stretching out her empty hands.

'She might have been just going to take the jug or have just given it up. I remember that both seemed to pause for an instant, as in a motion picture,' wrote Dr Jourdain.

The two Oxford ladies went on their way and soon reached a pavilion which stood in the middle of an enclosure. The place had a god-forsaken air about it and the atmosphere was depressing and unpleasant.

A man was sitting outside the pavilion, his face repulsively disfigured by smallpox, wearing a coat and a straw hat. He seemed not to notice the two women; at any rate he paid no attention to them.

Suddenly a young man in a dark coat and buckle shoes appeared and ran past shouting something like, 'You can't go through there.' He pointed towards the right and added, 'You'll find the house over there.'

Although the Englishwomen spoke French they could only partly understand the man's speech. He bowed with a curious smile and disappeared. The sound of his hurrying footsteps hung in the air for a long time.

The Englishwomen walked on in silence and after a while reached a narrow, rustic bridge, which led over a ravine. A small waterfall made its way between stones and fern leaves, down a slope covered in vegetation. On the other side of the bridge, the path wound along the edge of a meadow surrounded by trees. Some way away stood a small country house with shuttered windows and with terraces on either side. A lady was sitting on the lawn with her back to the house. She held a large sheet of paper or cardboard in her hand and seemed to be working at or looking at a drawing. She was no longer in the bloom of youth but looked most attractive. She wore a summer dress with a long bodice and a very full, apparently short skirt, which was extremely unusual. She had a pale green fichu or kerchief draped around her shoulders, and a large white hat covered her fair hair.

At the end of the terraces was a second house. As the two women drew near a door suddenly flew open and slammed shut again. A young man with the demeanour of a servant, but not wearing livery, came out. As the two Englishwomen thought they had trespassed on private property, they followed the man towards the Petit Trianon. Quite unexpectedly, from one moment to the next, they found themselves in the middle of a crowd – apparently a wedding party – all dressed in the fashions of 1901.

The two Englishwomen took the coach from the palace back to their hotel and started their journey home.

On their return to England, Annie Moberley and Eleanor Jourdain discussed their trip and began to wonder about their experiences at the Petit Trianon. It transpired that although Annie Moberley had seen the lady with the sheet of paper in the meadow, Eleanor Jourdain had not. Annie Moberley, on the other hand, had seen neither the plough outside the abandoned farm, nor the woman and the girl. Both Englishwomen naturally assumed that they had each seen the same things. Since this was evidently not the case, they decided to investigate the matter in detail. They analysed the events of the afternoon of 10 August 1901 at the Petit Trianon – the unusual costume of the people they had met and the inexplicable uneasiness which had overcome them. After comparing notes they decided to gather all the available information about the Petit Trianon in an attempt to find an explanation.

In July 1904 the two Englishwomen returned to Versailles. They discovered that the cottage outside which Dr Jourdain had seen the woman and the girl looked totally different. And the place where they had met the two men in eighteenth-century costume was also completely changed. The path on which the man had shown them the way was no longer to be found, in fact all the features of the landscape seemed to have changed. There was no wooden bridge and no waterfall, and in the place where they had seen the lady sitting in the meadow a bush was growing. The house on the terraces, too, did not remotely resemble the one which they had seen three years before.

Faced with all these anomalies, the Englishwomen decided to undertake a systematic investigation. The task took them several years. They procured old maps and plans of Versailles and its surroundings, examined documents in the Bibliothèque Nationale in Paris and enlisted the help of historians. Gradually a clearer picture began to emerge as many details could be explained or accounted for.

The plough which Eleanor Jourdain had seen, for example, did not belong to the Petit Trianon, but there were records to show that it had once been kept there and had been sold after the French Revolution.

In eighteenth-century Versailles, the only people who wore green livery were royal servants at Versailles. The two men in green coats could be identified as the Bersy brothers, who had been on watch on 5 October 1789, the last day which Marie-Antoinette spent at the Petit Trianon.

The cottage was shown on an old map near the entrance to the Petit Trianon. And a general plan of Versailles in the year 1783 showed that a round pavilion with pillars had existed around the time of the French Revolution, as well as the still existing Temple d'Amour.

Both the girl and the pock-marked man were identified from historical sources. The fourteen-year-old girl was the gardener's daughter, Marion, and the man with a straw hat over his pock-marked face was Count de Vaudreuil, a Creole, who had played a significant part in the downfall of Marie-Antoinette. In 1789, the sombrero was just coming into fashion.

The running man with the buckle shoes must have been de Bretagne, a page who according to historical sources was sent by the palace's major-domo to the Trianon with an urgent message for the queen. He was to tell Marie-Antoinette to escape immediately, as the mob was already on its way to Versailles from Paris.

The door which had banged shut behind the servant had been nailed up since the French Revolution. The man was possibly Lagrange, the doorkeeper.

The Englishwomen also discovered from the historical sources that the queen had been in the gardens on 5 October 1789 when the messenger brought her the news that she should return directly to the Trianon, from where she could be brought to safety. Having delivered his message, the man ran straight off to fetch a coach.

The archives even contained the name of the dressmaker who worked for the queen. She was called Madame Eloff, and it appeared that in the year 1789 she had made two green silk fichus for Marie-Antoinette.

In 1902, Annie Moberley happened to set eyes on a portrait of the queen painted by Wertmüller and was amazed to find that it had the features of the lady in the meadow near the Trianon.

In her account of this sudden appearance of a landscape from another century, Annie Moberley said: 'Everything suddenly looked unnatural, therefore unpleasant; even the trees behind the building seemed to have become flat and lifeless, like a wood worked in tapestry. There were no effects of light and shade, and no wind stirred the trees. It was all intensely still.'

Dr Jourdain had evidently received a similar impression: 'The whole scene – sky, trees and buildings – gave a little shiver.'

We must now consider how the Englishwomen's strange experience can be explained. There are several alternatives.

Possibly the most obvious is that on touring the grounds of the palace they were unconsciously reminded of historical events which they had once read or heard about, and these, triggered off by the surroundings, unfolded in their mind's eye. However, it seems a remarkable coincidence that they should both have had such an experience simultaneously, albeit in a slightly different form.

Another possibility is that the Englishwomen invented the whole story purely in order to attract attention. But this can probably be discounted in view of the fact that the publication of the events at the Petit Trianon only took place many years later, and both Annie Moberley and Eleanor Jourdain were women of great personal integrity.

A further explanation would be that the two of them experienced a day-dream. However, this can surely be excluded on the grounds that it would be too much of a coincidence for them both to have dreamed about the same thing at the same time and in the same place. Unless, of course, one supposes that either consciously or unconsciously they each influenced one another.

There is one further explanation, albeit a rather far-fetched one, and this is that the two Englishwomen for some unknown reason were displaced into another temporal dimension in which a fragment of this past era appeared before them.

It is interesting to note that on 10 August 1901, the day of their experience, electrical storms were recorded over Europe and the atmosphere was laden with static electricity. Could this have led to an alteration in the local 'temporal field' around Versailles, or is such an idea altogether too far-fetched?

On the afternoon of 4 September 1953 around 3.30 p.m. a Londoner by the name of C. W. Bradley was watching an exciting television programme. He could hardly believe his

eyes when the American call-sign KLEE-TV suddenly
appeared on the screen in the middle of the transmission.
Bradley racked his brains as to the meaning of this apparition
but could find no rational explanation. He was not the only
one to see it, however; later in the same month the same
letters appeared on the display screens of Atlantic Electronics
Ltd, in Lancashire.

The reception of stray TV signals from overseas
transmitters is not normally a cause for alarm, but in this case
it was certainly strange. The call-sign KLEE-TV had last
been transmitted three years previously, having been replaced by another programme sign in July 1950. Since that time
no transmitter on earth had sent the letters KLEE-TV into
the ether.

No satisfactory explanation was ever found for this occurrence, though widely differing theories were put forward.
Some people suggested that plasma clouds (consisting of
ionized gas) could have stored the signal for some unknown
reason and then released it again after the appropriate
period, others that the phenomenon was due to extraterrestrial influences.

Just as the American call-sign suddenly appeared from
nowhere, an airliner full of passengers disappeared under
similar circumstances to the Minuteman missile. It was in
1969 that an incoming commercial aircraft created a sensation in the control tower of Miami airport. The fully laden
machine was approaching the runway from a north-easterly
direction. It was under air-traffic control and was being
followed on the radar screens. Suddenly, the aircraft disappeared without a trace, only to reappear just as suddenly
ten minutes later. The landing took place without further
incident, and the pilot and crew were surprised by the
apparently unreasonable excitement of the ground staff.
When one of the radar operators told them that their
machine had disappeared for nearly ten minutes, all the

crew's watches and the clocks on board the aircraft were checked, and were found to be ten minutes slow. This was particularly inexplicable in view of the fact that a time-check with the control tower twenty minutes before the occurrence had shown them all to be correct.

Like the Minuteman, this machine must have disappeared for some inexplicable reason into another temporal dimension. But where to? Obviously neither the passengers nor the crew had undergone any change, in fact they had not even noticed the occurrence. Only the clocks had reacted.

Professor J. A. Wheeler of Princeton University in the United States, one of the few real experts on Einstein's theory of relativity and a co-inventor of the hydrogen bomb, believes that a kind of super-space exists side by side with our own universe. According to Wheeler, in this super-space both time and speed have lost their validity. In this indescribable world the word time can no longer be used in the usual sense, and the words 'before' and 'afterwards' have no meaning.

Perhaps the Minuteman and the airliner were, for reasons unknown to us, transported out of our own dimension into this super-space.

The English philosopher and mathematician Professor Alfred North Whitehead (1861–1947) was evidently aware of just how little we really know about the phenomenon of time when he wrote: 'It is impossible to reflect on time and the creative unfolding of nature, without becoming painfully aware of the limitations of human intelligence.'

Even without having recourse to Wheeler's super-space, it will be obvious from the following example how relative the concept of time and the words 'past', 'present' and 'future' really are.

Light in a vacuum has a speed of about 300,000 km per second. The distance it can travel in a year is known as a light-year. The star Rigel is 880 light-years away from us. If we look at it through a telescope in the night sky, we see it not as it is now, but as it was 880 years ago. Let us assume that Rigel has a planetary system, and suppose that one of these planets is inhabited by a highly developed civilization which has decided to investigate our solar system. Its astronomers have a super-telescope which enables them to observe life on earth in the smallest detail. Now instead of seeing aeroplanes, skyscrapers, mushroom clouds, they would see the earth in the year AD 1098 – two years after the first crusaders left Normandy for Jerusalem, and a year before they first conquered the holy city for Christendom.

If the inhabitants of the Rigel system wanted to observe the year 1978 on our earth, they would have to wait 880 years – i.e. until the year AD 2858 in our calendar. Likewise an earthly astronomer observing Rigel today would, for the inhabitants of the Rigel system, be a man from the future, in other words a future event.

But it is not only astronomers who have access to the past. The Canadian neurosurgeon Wilder Penfield succeeded in capturing the past in an entirely different way, and without involving himself in astronomical distances.

Penfield succeeded in dividing the personality of his experimental subjects into two. During his experiments, one half of the subject's personality lived in the present while the other was transported back into the past. Penfield located the area in the brain where suppressed feelings and memories are stored. By stimulating the area with electrodes, these can be brought back into immediate consciousness.

For medical reasons, Penfield had to carry out over a thousand brain operations under local anaesthetic. One of the patients he treated in this way was a Dutch woman who had emigrated to Canada. During the operation she lay on the operating table fully conscious, with an opening in her skull. When Penfield stimulated her brain with electrodes she suddenly started talking about Christmas Eve 1945, in Amsterdam. Her memory was clear and precise in every detail, despite the fact that the experience had remained inaccessible to her immediate consciousness for many years. In other experiments Penfield made a female patient count the bricks on a wall which formed the background to a scene she re-experienced during the course of an operation. As the wall in question was still standing at the time of the experiment, it was possible to verify that the number of bricks given by the patient was absolutely correct.

Thus, according to Penfield, the past can be brought to life again by electrical stimulation of a particular area of the brain.

Penfield's experiments would also explain why we can sometimes relive events long past in our dreams in every detail. Our past, in fact, is like a three-dimensional sound film, biochemically stored in our memory.

According to a recent theory, during dreaming our daily experiences are compared with this 'sound film of our past', so that the new experiential data can be mastered and correctly classified. This is why in our dreams the daily events of our lives are very often mixed with long-forgotten experiences from our past.

7

In Pursuit of an Archetype

Probably the oldest recorded dreams and their interpretations are to be found in the ancient Babylonian *Epic of Gilgamesh,* which originated some 2000 years BC. The Nineveh version of the Gilgamesh poem goes back to about 1200 BC and was found about 140 years ago among more than 20,000 different texts, incised on clay tablets, which lay buried under the ruins of the library of ancient Nineveh. The inscriptions were in Akkadian – the scholarly language of king Assurbanipal's court – and were not deciphered until much later. And it was many years after this that scholars finally translated the *Epic of Gilgamesh,* a poem of over 300 exquisitely melancholy quatrains celebrating the fabulous life of the Sumerian king Gilgamesh.

The *Epic of Gilgamesh* was originally part of the cultural heritage of all the Oriental nations and was translated into many different languages. In it Gilgamesh is glorified as a descendant of the gods, a native of Uruk, which is mentioned (as Erech) in the Old Testament. The story tells of Gilgamesh's ancestor, Utnapishtim, the only immortal being on earth, and of Gilgamesh's long and adventure-filled journey with Enkidu, his friend from the steppes, in search of eternal life and the way to overcome death.

Enkidu opened his mouth and spoke to Gilgamesh:
'Shall we find the trail of Humbaba (an enemy warrior) thus?
Let us look at some dreams, one after the other.
May the dreams be threefold' . . .
They both decided to take their evening rest;
Sleep, springing from the night, overcame them.
In the middle of the night, he (Gilgamesh) gave forth a dream.
He related the dream to Enkidu:
'Friend, what is this? Did you not disturb me?
Why am I awake?
We stood in deep rocky chasms,
The mountain was falling down. . .,
It dashed me to the ground,
It seized my feet and would not let them go.
Before its might we were like flies in a bank of reeds.
There was a strong and blinding light, a man appeared to me,
The most handsome in the land, great was his beauty.
He drew me down under the mountain. . .
Soaked me with water, my heart grew tender,
He gave me ground under my feet. . .'
He who was borne on the steppes . . . Enkidu,
Spoke to his friend, Enkidu explained the dream:
'Your dream, friend, is beautiful, the dream is delightful. . .
Friend, the mountain which you saw is Humbaba!
We will catch Humbaba, kill him,
And throw his corpse out onto the plain.
Tomorrow everything will be accomplished!' . . .

But Gilgamesh climbed up to the mountain,
Scattered his flour on the mountain:
'Mountain, bring me a dream, a word from Shamash the sun god!'

And it gave him one, and to Enkidu . . .
While Gilgamesh was sitting there, his head resting on his
leg,
He was overcome by the sleep which flows down upon
men.
In the middle watch he broke off his sleep,
Got up and said to his friend:
'Friend, did you not call me? Why am I awake
Did you not touch me? Why am I filled with horror?
Did not a god pass by? Why are my limbs trembling?
Friend, I saw a third dream,
And the dream which I saw was quite horrifying:
The heavens shrieked, the earthly kingdom roared
. . . was struck still, darkness came forth,
lightning flashed, a fire blazed up,
. . . became more and more intense, death rained down.
Suddenly the white-hot fire went out,
And that which fell down, was turned to ashes.'

Unfortunately some sections containing Enkidu's interpretation are missing, but it can be assumed that he explained
this dream as well as he had the previous one. The whole of
Gilgamesh's adventure-filled journey is reminiscent of a
shaman's dream. In the Underworld, for example, the
goddess Inanna makes a drum and drumstick for Gilgamesh
from the roots of a willow. As in shamanism, the main theme
of the *Epic of Gilgamesh* is the mastery of the Underworld and
death, and in both cases dreaming plays a central role. The
appearance of shamanistic influence here is hardly surprising, since it goes back to the very roots of mankind.

Even older records of dreams than the *Epic of Gilgamesh* are to
be found in prehistoric caves. Early man demonstrated his
powers of imagination in his cave paintings, which are
nothing less than the picture book of his dreams.

The well known Polish émigré mathematician and anthropologist Professor Jacob Bronowski (1908–1976) commented on the prehistoric cave paintings in his book *The Ascent of Man:*

I think that the power that we see expressed here for the first time is the power of anticipation: the forward-looking imagination. In these paintings the hunter was made familiar with dangers which he knew he had to face but to which he had not yet come. When the hunter was brought here into the secret dark and the light was suddenly flashed on the pictures, he saw the bison as he would have to face him, he saw the running deer, he saw the turning boar... For us, the cave paintings re-create the hunter's way of life as a glimpse of history; we look through them into the past. But for the hunter, I suggest, they were a peep-hole into the future; he looked ahead. In either direction, the cave paintings act as a kind of telescope tube of the imagination: they direct the mind from what is seen to what can be inferred or conjectured.

In fact the motifs of the cave paintings include not only hunting scenes but also typical dream symbols. These are to be found in caves all over the world – in France, Spain, Siberia, Africa, China, Japan, South America and Australia. In the caves at Altamira (Spain) and Ussat, Ariège and Pair-non-Pair (France), for example, curious disc-shaped or oval forms are to be found above the paintings of prehistoric animals. They are strongly reminiscent of airships and present-day descriptions of UFOs, which C. G. Jung maintained were typical dream symbols or archetypes.

A friend of C. G. Jung had the following dream on 27 May 1957:

'It was late afternoon or early evening. The sun sank, a red disc with sharp outlines, behind a transparent veil of cloud. Glaring white light. Suddenly it faded into a pallor which spread in a horrifying manner over the whole of the western horizon. The ashen daylight changed into an emptiness which filled me with horror. Then a second sun appeared in the west. Starting as a disc, it turned into a clearly recognizable sphere – a ball.

'As the sun went down and darkness fell, the ball came at breakneck speed towards the earth. With nightfall the atmosphere of the dream changed completely. The night sky became overpowering and respect and fear flowed into me. It seemed to be shrouded in a thin veil of clouds. Here and there a star shone faintly through.

'At first, as the ball approached the earth at a furious speed, I thought that Jupiter must have fallen out of its orbit. But then I noticed that despite its size it was still far too small for a planet like Jupiter. As the ball came closer, definite patterns became recognizable on its surface. But they were more symbolic than geographical or geometric in character. I was transfixed by the beauty of this greyish-white ball against the background of the night sky. Everyone who had gathered to watch followed the approach of the ball in dread, for a collision with the earth seemed inevitable. But at the same time we were conscious of the fact that we were watching a cosmic event, and this aroused our astonishment and wonder. While we were watching this drama in fascination, more and more balls suddenly appeared, approaching us at an uncanny speed. Each of them burst with a fearful explosion, but they were so far from us that we could not make out how they had been detonated. Just once, I thought I saw a streak of lightning. The balls kept bursting all around us, but always so far away from us that we could not see what damage they were causing. We did not dare to go nearer as we were afraid of being hit.

'Later I went home. There I saw myself in conversation with a young woman. She was sitting in a basket chair writing busily in a notebook. We all wanted to move to some other, safer area. I think we went south-west. I asked the young woman whether she wouldn't prefer to come with us, but she firmly refused. Strictly speaking the danger was just as great everywhere, and I admired the young woman for her logic and intelligence in coming to this decision.

'Towards the end of my dream I met another young woman. Perhaps it was the same one as before. She was sitting in her chair, absorbed in her work, with a self-confident and competent air. In fact she was bigger and more attractive than the first, and I also saw her face. She spoke to me directly and distinctly, using my full name. Her exact words were: "You will live till 11.08." She said these eight words – there were exactly eight, with my Christian name and sur-names – in such an authoritarian manner that I felt somehow guilty of doubting that I would live only till eight minutes past eleven.'

Jung was not interested in whether UFOs are a real phenomenon or not. The question of whether there are extra-terrestrial spaceships was not the crucial point. For Jung, UFOs were a genuine, religious experience. He saw in them the circular eye of God – the symbol of completeness, of divinity. For him they represented a psychic projection, the vision of an archetypal symbol of completeness. He took the view that the world-wide accounts of UFOs were evidence of a universal psychic disposition. 'But according to Freud flying saucers in sexual fantasies are the womb,' he commented angrily of his former teacher.

7 January 1948, 14.56 hours.
Excitement reigns in control room of Godman US Air

Force Base. The highway police have just announced the sighting of an unusual round flying object with a fiery red halo. The telephone shrills a second time and the military post at Fort Knox reports the same thing. The army administrative centre at Lexington confirms the sighting, and the base commander feels justified in sending up four Air National Guard F 51s to have a look.

The mission commander is Captain Thomas Mantell, an experienced fighter pilot with over 3600 flying hours behind him. His orders are to intercept the unknown aircraft and destroy it if necessary. One of Mantell's three back-up machines drops out with a technical fault.

Meanwhile the strange phenomenon is being watched not only by hundreds of people in Madisonville, Kentucky, but by thousands of Americans all over the country. The telephones are jammed with enquiries.

14.56 The machines take off almost vertically with a thunderous roar. Soon they are out of sight. Radar screens take over their observation.

15.00 Mantell comes in on the radio:
Nothing in sight. Flying in direction of Ohio River Falls. Out.

15.02 Visibility 100 per cent. Not a thing in sight.
Flying height 28,000 feet. Still climbing. Out.

15.09 Reached 28,000 feet. Nothing in sight.

15.11 Mantell here. Now I've got it! It's a disc, enormously large. Hard to say, could be 80 yards in diameter. Upper surface has a ring and a dome. Turning fantastically fast, apparently round a central vertical axis. My altimeter reads 31,500 feet. Out.

In the control room all hell is let loose. The giant disc has suddenly appeared on the radar screen. Everyone scrambles to get a look.

15.12 Call from the right wing pilot:
I can see the disc. Am photographing it.
Mantell's behind. About 200 feet above me.
Left wing pilot falling in.
Attempting to pursue.

15.14 Call from Mantell:
Another thousand yards and I've got it.
Flying twice as fast. I'm overtaking the thing. It's got a
metallic gleam. It's shrouded in yellowish light – now
the colour's changing, becoming reddish – orange-
coloured.

15.15 Just 400 yards to go. Disc speeding up. Trying to
escape. Climbing at about 45 degrees. Out.

15.16 Right wing pilot:
Mantell's almost got it, only a couple of yards more.
Disc is putting on a spurt. Can't keep up. Out.

15.18 Mantell: The thing's gigantic. It's flying unbelievably
fast. I can see windows. Now . . .

The wing pilots ask permission to land as Mantell has
disappeared into the cloud cover.

Around four in the afternoon a search party found fragments
of Mantell's machine – strewn over a radius of nearly a mile.

Did Mantell – an experienced combat pilot – have a
daydream and go chasing after a Jungian archetype which
had cost him his life? He wasn't the only one to see the 'thing',
however, so if it was a dream, everyone must have had it,
including the radar equipment.

What exactly was the UFO?

The official attempts at an explanation read like a
gourmet's menu of exotic ideas. We can take our pick: it was a
fraud, a natural phenomenon, an illusion, a sighting of the
planet Venus, a mental aberration. Was Mantell chasing
after a skyhook – a reconnaissance balloon? Or was he really

following an extraterrestrial spaceship? Was the object which
swept past him the same as that which a prehistoric painter
had shown flying above a human figure on the wall of a cave
at Pech-Merle in France?

Perhaps the cave painter had had the same experience as
the natives and Europeans of the Anglican mission at Boainai
on the island of New Guinea in 1959 – an occurrence which
still occupies the minds of UFO researchers, and officials of
Western governments, today.

Boaini, 27–28 June 1959.

From the notes of the Reverend William Bruce Gill, an
Anglican priest and head of the mission, and a graduate of
Brisbane University. The Rev. Gill reported:

. . . and as I was about to turn around the corner of the
house, something caught my eye in the sky, and I looked up
toward the west. And there I saw at an angle of about 45
degrees this huge light. I didn't think, of course, even then
of flying saucers as such. I thought, well perhaps some
people could imagine these things, but never me. And
there it was. I called Eric Kodawara, and I said, 'What do
you see up there?'

He said, 'There seems to be a light.'

I said, 'Well, you go and tell the teacher Steven Moi.
Tell him to come along quickly.'

And then Eric went along, and he collected as many
people as he could, and we all stood and gazed at it. Then
we went further up into the playing field, and the
sighting went on. I've got it recorded here. I had decided
by this time very quickly to get a notebook and pencil, and
I thought, well, if anything is going to happen, it's going to
happen now, and surely tomorrow I'll wake up and think
it's been a dream, that I haven't really seen one. If I've got
it down here in pencil, then I'll know at least I haven't been
dreaming.

And here are the Reverend Gill's notes:

Time 6.45 p.m. sky: patches of low clouds. Sighted bright white light, direction northwest.
6.50 called Steven and Eric.
6.52 Steven arrived confirms, not star.
6.55 send Eric to call people. One object on top moving – man? Now three men – moving, glowing, doing something on deck. Gone.
7.00 men 1 and 2 again.
7.04 gone again.
7.10 sky cloud ceiling covered sky height about 2000 feet. Man 1, 3, 4, 2, (appeared in that order) thin electric blue spotlight. Men gone, spotlight still there.
7.12 men 1 and 2 appeared blue light.
7.20 spotlight off, men go.
7.20 UFO goes through cloud.
8.28 clear sky here, heavy cloud over Dogura. UFO seen by me overhead. Called station people. Appeared to descend, get bigger.
8.29 second UFO seen over sea – hovering at times.
8.35 another over Wadobuna Village.
8.50 clouds forming again. Big one stationary and larger. Others coming and going through clouds. As they descend through cloud, light reflected like large halo on to cloud – no more than 2000 feet, probably less. All UFOs very clear. 'Mother' ship still large, clear, stationary.
9.05 clouds patchy, numbers 2, 3, 4 gone.
9.10 number 1 gone overhead into cloud.
9.20 'Mother' back.
9.30 'Mother' gone, gone across sea toward Giwa.
9.46 Overhead UFO reappears, is hovering.
10.00 still stationary.
10.10 hovering, gone behind cloud.

10.30 very high hovering in clear patch of sky between clouds.

10.50 very overcast, no sign of UFO.

11.04 heavy rain.

Data sheet of observation of UFOs 6.45–11.04 p.m. Signed William B. Gill.

The Reverend Gill also gave the following account:

7.12, men 1 and 2 appeared – blue light. I might mention here that the cloud ceiling was about 2000 feet, and I judged the cloud ceiling by a mountain. And all of this, of course, was well under the cloud ceiling. By this time in a space of twenty-five minutes, the sky had clouded over. At 7.20 the UFO went through the clouds, right through. At 8.28 the sky was beginning to clear again, although it was heavy, the cloud cover was heavy over Giwa. UFO seen by me now over it. I called the station people the second time that night around twenty-eight minutes past eight, and it appeared to descend and get bigger. . . Others were coming and going through the clouds – remember we now had patches of clouds. They were descending through the clouds and the glow of the discs was reflected at the base of the clouds, and then they would go in through the cloud again, and they seemed to enjoy doing that.

Then came the next night, and this was the interesting one. A large UFO was first sighted by one of the nurses at the hospital at 6.00 p.m. . . . . It happened this way: we were walking, and this thing came down to what we estimated was the closest we had seen it, and was practically the closest we were ever to see it. Somewhere between 300 and 500 feet it dropped down. It was not dark, and we could see it quite clearly. It was still bright and sparkling, but it seemed very near and clear. And there was this figure again on the decking, as I called it, at the top. And it was the teacher who said, 'I wonder if it is going to land on the playing field.' I said, 'why not?' And so we waved, like that, – Hello – and we were a bit surprised now, and the thing waved back. And then Eric, who was with me, my constant companion, waved his two arms, along with another lad, and then the figures waved two arms back.

The Reverend Gill reported that Ananias Rarata and himself then continued to wave, and the figures on the deck of the UFO waved back, much to the joy of the people at the mission.

When it got dark, Gill called for a torch and started sending long, slow flashes towards the deck of the flying object. After a while the craft began to swing backwards and forwards in reply.

These events were observed by thirty-eight witnesses, twenty-five of whom signed William Bruce Gill's report. Amongst them were five teachers and three medical assistants.

Around the same time a large number of similar sightings were made over Papua, and were reported by the Reverend Norman E. G. Cruttwell, a member of the Anglican mission in Menapi, Papua. The first sighting from this period was made by the Director of Civil Aviation for the region of Papua, Mr T. P. Drury, who was stationed in Port Moresby.

The Reverend Gill wrote as follows:

The Boainai sightings climaxed a relatively short but remarkably acute period of UFO activity in the vicinity of eastern New Guinea. UFOs were observed by both Papuan natives and Europeans. Sightings were reported by educated Papuans and by totally illiterate natives relatively untouched by Western civilization and quite ignorant of 'flying saucers'.

Professor Allen Hynek, official astronomical adviser to the
US Air Force in connection with the latter's secret UFO
project Blue Book, and currently director of the Lindheimer
Astronomical Research Center at Northwestern University,
has the following comments to make on the sightings at
Boainai:

I first learned of the case in detail when I stopped at the
British Air Ministry on an official visit from Blue Book in
1961.

I learned at that time that the British military view of the
UFO problem was essentially the same as that of Blue
Book; indeed, the British (and other governments as well)
were looking to the US Air Force to solve the problem. I
was told quite bluntly that with the funds and facilities
available to the US Air Force there was little point to their
doing anything about the problem, and they honestly felt
that the US Air Force was doing something about it, but
with negative results.

The British Air Ministry did not take Father Gill's
sighting seriously, and almost with relief they gave me
their report on it; it had apparently been cluttering up
their files. Since then I have had access to a full report on
this case and have also been the recipient of a lengthy tape
recording of a talk by Reverend Gill and, more recently, of
an hour-long tape with Reverend Gill made by my
colleague Fred Beckman.

Before judgement is passed on this affair, Reverend Gill
should be heard. As a few excerpts from his tapes show,
Reverend Gill is utterly sincere. He talks in a leisurely,
scholarly way, delineating details slowly and carefully.
The manner and content of the tapes are conducive to
conviction. One would find it difficult to believe that an
Anglican priest would concoct a story involving more than
two dozen witnesses out of sheer intent to deceive. Critics of

this case do not generally know that this report is only one of some sixty in the New Guinea area at approximately that time, all investigated by a colleague of Gill, the Reverend Norman Cruttwell, who has written a report covering the series, only one of which, the case in point, involved humanoids.

However that may be, the Australian Air Ministry rejected the idea of a personal discussion with the Reverend Gill, although no report on the subject was available. It wrote to an official on the subject as follows:

CANBERRA, ACT
28 January 1970

Dear Sir,

I refer to your letter dated 12 November 1969 concerning an unusual aerial sighting at Boainai, in Papua, New Guinea. The RAAF could come to no definite conclusion on the report, and enquiries with the United Kingdom and the United States could add no clues or answers.

As a result these sightings have been classified as aerial phenomena, but most probably they were reflections on a cloud of a major light source of unknown origin.

Yours faithfully

In his book *The UFO Experience*, Hynek commented:

The letter is correct in one sense. When the brightly lighted UFO seen by Reverend Gill and his many colleagues went vertically upward, it illuminated the clouds as it passed through the overcast. The letter is quite correct, also, in stating that the light source was of unknown origin!

It must be admitted that there is a lot of hocus-pocus connected with so-called flying saucers. But even if we exclude all the cases where they have been confused with satellites, planets, balloons and aircraft, and other mis-identifications, if we lay aside the stories of commercially minded opportunists, confidence tricksters, swindlers and the like, there remains a percentage of UFO sightings which cannot be explained. Indeed, according to a study by the American Institute for Aeronautics and Astronautics, the largest space research organization in the world, the figure is as high as 30 per cent. And a high proportion of the in-numerable sightings made were by absolutely reliable and highly qualified observers, such as astronomers, astronauts, ships' captains, pilots, radar operators and meteorologists.

Many observers and so-called ufologists are convinced that the objects seen are in fact extraterrestrial spaceships.

Professor Carl Sagan, director of the Laboratory for Planetary Studies at Cornell University in the United States, does not take these UFO theories very seriously, although he is absolutely convinced of the existence of extraterrestrial life. Sagan is one of the leading astronomers and exobiologists (exobiology = extraterrestrial biology) of our time and is highly unorthodox in his views. It was as a result of his encouragement that the *Pioneer 10* probe sent into space in 1972 was fitted with a gold-plated aluminium plaque bearing a picture of a naked human couple and binary number symbols. The idea was to inform any beings who might find the probe somewhere in interstellar space where the probe came from and who had made it.

It is not entirely impossible that the probe will be found by an extraterrestrial intelligence. In our own stellar system alone – the Milky Way – there are thousands of millions of stars with planets on which life could exist. Experts estimate that there are at least 6000 million stars with inhabitable planetary systems.

Thus it is entirely possible that the *Pioneer 10* probe will create a sensation in some other civilization a hundred light-years away, but at a speed of only 50,000 km an hour it would take no less than 2 million years to get there. And who knows whether by then our planet will still bear life, or whether it will be an atomic waste.

Sagan's argument against the possibility of UFOs being extraterrestrial spaceships runs roughly as follows:

Let us presuppose that there are a million stars with highly developed civilizations on their surrounding planetary systems, and take the most optimistic view that the life-span of such a technologically advanced civilization would be 10 million years. If each of these civilizations sent a single spaceship on a journey into space each year – each of which made contact with one other civilization in that year – that would mean that a million spaceships would arrive somewhere each year. The Milky Way has at least 10,000 million planets worth visiting (and there are at least 100,000 million stars in the Milky Way altogether). On this basis, for only a single UFO to reach the earth each year, each civilization would have to send out 10,000 spaceships. In other words, 10 million spaceships would have to leave their homes in the Milky Way each year.

Sagan's view is that this seems out of the question. For even if we imagine a civilization far in advance of our own, it would be asking far too much to assume that they send out 10,000 spaceships, only one of which reaches us.

In fact Sagan's argument seems hard to justify. Astronomically speaking there are only a few stars within a distance of 20 light-years from the earth with planets which could maintain intelligent life. In fact there are at the most nine stars far enough from each other to qualify, including binary and triple systems:

Alpha Centauri   4.3 light-years away

Epsilon Eridani	10.8 light-years away
Tau Ceti	11.8 light-years away
70 Ophiuchi	16.4 light-years away
Eta Cassiopeiæ	18.0 light-years away
Sigma Draconis	18.2 light-years away
36 Ophiuchi .	18.2 light-years away
H R 7703	18.6 light-years away
Delta Pavonis	19.2 light-years away

Let us assume that on a planet of the star Epsilon Eridani
there is an intelligent civilization far enough advanced to
undertake interstellar travel. It would be logical to assume
that such a civilization would start by looking for intelligent
life within the proximity of its own system, say up to 20 light-
years away. Including our own star, the Sun, there would be
nine such stars for them to consider. If they intended to visit
all nine stars they would need not 10,000 spaceships but nine.
And if they reached the Solar System with our planet Earth at
their first attempt, they would probably (if they were remotely
human in their ways of thinking) return to this same system
again and again.

   But even if we assume that a hypothetical, highly
developed civilization exists at a far greater distance – say 100
light-years – Sagan's argument would still fall down, since a
systematic scanning for radio signals would enable them to be
far more selective in their sending out of spaceships than he
suggests.

Neither Sagan's argument nor its refutation can really be used to confirm the hypothesis that UFOs are extra-terrestrial spaceships. Since one theory is as good as another in this context, UFOs could just as well be flying machines from the future. They could be time-travel machines invented by our descendants to investigate our own present.

The following episodes will serve to demonstrate that the idea is not totally outlandish.

In the last decade of the nineteenth century – in the years 1896 and 1897 – motorized aircraft appeared in many parts of the United States, although such a machine had not yet been invented at this time.

Thousands of people saw and described cigar-shaped or oval, dirigible flying objects with sails or wings, propellers or rotating fans, and searchlights, rear-lights and side-lights in brilliant red, green and blue. Occasionally noises were heard in connection with these flying objects, described variously as hissing, sizzling or droning. Their mode of progress was described by witnesses either as floating or flying. Estimates of their speed varied from very slow, about 5 mph (8 km an hour), to very fast, about 200 mph (320 km an hour).

The first flying object of this kind appeared in November 1896. Between January and the middle of March 1897 there was a pause, then the sightings resumed until May of the same year. Witnesses described these aircraft as being dirigible machines in the form of a cigar or cylinder. They were all driven by some form of motor – and were therefore by implication heavier-than-air machines. Confusion with captive balloons was out of the question, since the latter were very obviously rounded in shape with a basket for the passengers underneath.

At that time it was generally thought that air travel could most feasibly be achieved with airships, which are lighter than air, and not with motorized 'heavier-than-air' machines.

Naturally the sighting of a type of flying object which had not yet been invented caused a great stir. Witnesses who had observed these machines stated that they invariably seemed to give warning of their approach by strong, dazzling white or red searchlights, and these became known as a characteristic feature of their sudden appearances.

In Atkinson, Wisconsin, for example, observers saw a flying body with a white front and red tail light. These sources of light enabled the length of the flying object to be estimated at about 50 feet (15 m) and its flying height at about 500 feet (150 m).

In Everest, Kansas, a flying machine appeared one evening at about 21.05. It hovered above the town hall and swung its searchlight back and forth as if signalling to those below.

The editor-in-chief of the Texas daily, the *Edna Press*, saw two flying objects at the same time, which gave warning of their presence with coloured lights, one green and the other red.

And on 18 April 1897 the *Chicago Tribune* reported the sighting of a flying body equipped with wings or sails, some 17 feet (5 m) long and 20 feet (6 m) wide.

An aircraft was observed over Texas in a 'shining cloud of vapour'. A kind of wing was visible on either side of the cigar-shaped object, from which large 'rotating fans' projected to the front and behind at an angle of about 45 degrees. Observers estimated the 'bird-like' flying object to be about 200 feet long.

At Fort Worth in Texas, on the other hand, witnesses described an aircraft with bat-like wings which resembled a travelling coach with the front and rear ends tapering into a point.

In Guthrie, Oklahoma, eye-witnesses reported that a flying object had come down to earth and then immediately shot up vertically at enormous speed – much to the delight of the spectators – and disappeared into the night sky.

Generally speaking it was difficult to get exact estimates of the objects' speeds from witnesses. Most of them merely used such terms as 'very slow' or 'very fast'. But an engine driver from Burlington, Iowa, compared the speed of a flying object with that of his train and estimated it as 150 mph (240 km an hour).

That great German philosopher and misanthropist Arthur Schopenhauer (1788–1860) based his major work, *Die Welt als Wille und Vorstellung* ('The world as will and idea'), on a number of questions concerning our apprehension of reality: What justifies our claim that we have a correct knowledge of the exterior world? Under what circumstances do we achieve this knowledge? To what extent does reality correspond to our concept of it and our belief? What relationship is there between ourselves as experienced individuals and the reality which we maintain that we know?

Schopenhauer came to the conclusion that the idea of an objective reality, independent of our will and our own conception of it, is not possible.

In order to understand his point more clearly, let us envisage twenty painters all painting the same model. Each of them has a different conception of the model – he sees it so to speak with his own eyes. The result is twenty different portraits of the same model. But each individual portrait is reality for the artist who has painted it. We can even go a step further and say that each painter has projected his own reality into the model.

As we have already seen, for C. G. Jung even UFOs were a projected form of reality – a psychic projection by the observer. This problem was one which occupied him even in his dreams. In 1959 he had a dream in which he saw two lens-shaped, gleaming metallic discs which flew over his house in a shallow curve and then veered off down towards the sea. Immediately afterwards another flying object came directly towards him. It was a completely round lens, looking like the objective of a telescope. When it was some 120 to 150 m (130 to 160 yards) away it halted and remained motionless in the air for a moment, then flew on. Immediately afterwards another object shot straight over him. This time it was a lens with a metallic extension leading to a box – a magic lantern. Some 180 to 210 m (195 to 230 yards) away the object stopped dead, pointing straight at Jung. He woke up with a feeling of amazement. While he was still half dreaming, the thought passed through his mind: 'We always think that UFOs are our projections. Now it turns out that we are their projections. I am projected as Carl Gustav Jung by the magic lantern. But who is using the apparatus?'

8

Cycles of Activity

We have all had the experience of being lost in thought, unaware of our surroundings, only to be brought to ourselves by some such comment as, 'What are you doing? Day-dreaming?' Perhaps scenes from our last holiday were passing through our mind, or we were imagining ourselves with a loved one. Or we may well have been venting our anger on a superior, and telling him in no uncertain terms what we thought of him. Day-dreaming is something which we have all done at some time or other.

The American writer and philosopher Prentice Mulford (1834–1891) once said: 'Every imagining is an invisible reality, and the longer, the more intensely it is held on to, the more of it will be transformed into that form of being which can be felt, seen, touched, perceived.'

This view has been confirmed by a twenty-year study carried out by Jerome L. Singer, a psychologist at Yale University. Through his researches Singer was able to prove that day-dreams are a part of our most basic modes of behaviour. He maintained that they go far beyond the resolution of conflicts caused by sexual or aggressive drives, affording intense pleasure and relieving boredom or frustration. It also transpired from Singer's experiments that the fantasies we have in day-dreams can be regarded as a means of exploring future behaviour, a medium through which we can examine future possibilities without becoming involved in a course of action which may have unforeseeable results. Singer concluded that usually day-dreams clearly reflect persons, objects and events, and that visual images are the predominant medium for fantasy experiences. We are most likely to fall into a day-dream when we are alone, but some of Singer's subjects admitted to day-dreaming constantly, even in social situations.

Thus, dreams take possession of us, not only at night but during the daytime also.

Singer's finding that day-dreams should be regarded as an exploration of modes of behaviour echoes Jouvet's view that REM dreaming is a training ground for instinctive behaviour. This startling coincidence suggests an interesting possibility – that the waking person may, like the sleeping one, experience something like the succession of REM and non-REM phases.

Singer and his colleagues wondered whether it would be possible to glean some information about the nature of day-dreams from the subject's eye movements. However, since in our normal waking state, any complex environment will cause our eyes to move rapidly and very frequently, any experiment on the relationship between thinking patterns and eye movements is fraught with difficulty.

The first experiments were conducted on female subjects. They were asked to lie down on a couch in an empty, darkened room. In order to reproduce the atmosphere in which day-dreaming takes place as accurately as possible and maintain a degree of visual stimulation, street noises and the play of light and shadow through exterior windows were not excluded. The subjects were connected to an EEG apparatus which recorded their brain waves and eye movements. After any continuous period without eye movement or with rapid eye movements, they had to relate what had been happening. They were given mental stimuli on previously established themes, being asked to imagine specific events with open or closed eyes. For example they had to imagine that they were watching a man on a trampoline, or a tennis match, or think of the latest developments in arithmetic. One particularly interesting suggestion was that they should induce a day-dream involving 'the fulfilment of secret wishes' which 'no one except the subject knew anything about'. First of all they were asked to indulge totally in the fulfilment of these wishes, then in the next experiment they had to let these secret, unfulfilled desires rise to the surface again, only to banish them immediately from their consciousness. In other words they were obliged deliberately to suppress an already existing fantasy.

The results of these experiments proved highly fruitful in a number of ways. It appeared from the reports made by the subjects that fantasies or day-dreams begin shortly after a period without eye movement. Rapid and frequent eye movements, on the other hand, were characteristic of active and conscious sequences of thought. Descriptions of scenes and situations in the day-dreams were also associated with eye movements. The subjects' eyes remained relatively still when they were preoccupied with their secret desires, but a whole series of rapid eye movements was provoked when they were attempting to suppress them. The experiments showed that a day-dream or visual fantasy could only be induced in a waking state if the external environment was deliberately excluded.

A further experiment with young men confirmed the theory that eye movement is greater when there is suppression of thought than with the most lively fantasies. When asked to suppress a desire, the subjects tended to look round the room with eyes wide open, as if to erase the contents of the fantasy by deliberately feeding in fresh visual stimuli. Just as characteristic eye movements accompany the REM and non-REM phases of nocturnal sleep, so particular eye movements characterize the phases of day-dreaming.

The American sleep researcher Dr Julius Segal raised some interesting questions in this connection in the book *Sleep and Dreams*, written in collaboration with Gay Luce. Segal writes:

> If a biological tide, a discharge of excitement in the brain's centres of drive, rises and ebbs roughly every ninety minutes during sleep, could we also see it by day? Is this 'dream period' we see so clearly in the quiescence of nightly sleep a life-long clock, continually charging and recharging our drive centres? Is this a basic motor for our motivation, causing the lazy animal to get up from his rest before his stomach pains begin and search for food, urging the male to search out a mate – a system that periodically jolts us into alertness, pushing us to exert ourselves to survive?

There is a great deal of evidence to suggest that periods similar to the REM phases occur throughout the daytime. In healthy men, for example, erections occur during the nocturnal REM phase and continue to do so into old age. The same waves of excitement are also found in women, whose clitoris becomes erect. Amazingly enough, these unconsciously regulated swellings and contractions of the penis and clitoris continue in a ninety-minute rhythm throughout the day. But as these 'waves of potency' are much weaker during the daytime, they are less easily noticed.

An experiment carried out in Mount Sinai Hospital in New York helps to confirm that our organism is subject to a constant cycle of activity. At Mount Sinai, Charles Fisher and Stanley Friedman tested the need for food and refreshment in normal people. Ten people were isolated for a day in a hospital room which contained a generous supply of food and refreshments. Each of the subjects was allowed to eat, drink and smoke as much as he wished. Light reading matter was also provided. A points system was devised to score the intake of individual subjects. Thus a sandwich scored eight points, a can of beer eight points, a cigarette three points, and so on.

An observer sat concealed behind a two-way mirror, noting every item which disappeared between the lips of the subjects throughout the day. Their consumption was nothing short of astounding.

Eight of the ten participants displayed a fluctuating cycle of need lasting from eighty to 120 minutes, irrespective of hunger contractions in their stomachs. Hunger contractions only appeared from two and a half to four and a half hours after a meal. The subjects' periodic urges to eat, drink and smoke suggested that there was a cycle of activity in the area of the brain controlling appetite, similar to the REM phases of sleep.

Industrial physiologists have established that workers' performance and factory accidents are also subject to cycles. The first increase in accidents at work places takes place around 10 a.m. There is a second wave around 1 p.m. in which accidents become even more frequent, and the accident rate is highest of all in the evening around 5 p.m. After the tea and lunch breaks, at 10 a.m. and 1 p.m. respectively, output increases again.

In England, similar experiments produced the same results. The work performance of secretaries was scrutinized in a number of government offices and businesses, and it was discovered that most typing errors were made around 10 a.m., 1 p.m. and 5 p.m. After the tea and lunch breaks at 10 a.m. and 1 p.m., there was again an increase in performance.

A number of German factories attempted to capitalize on

these results by introducing gymnastics at the 10 o'clock break. The intention was to reduce industrial accidents during the critical periods, and indeed the employees are reported to be psychologically more balanced than before.

Traffic accidents follow the same temporal rhythm, with critical periods occurring once again at 10 a.m., 1 p.m. and 5 p.m. The cycle of accidents at night time follows a similar pattern, most of them occurring around 1 a.m., 3 a.m. and 5 a.m. It is worth noting that drivers who get up at 3 in the morning are just as prone to accidents as those who have been on the road since midnight. Thus it is not the number of hours which a driver has spent behind the wheel which counts, but his degree of wakefulness, which increases and diminishes in a cyclic pattern.

We know that humans, mammals and birds experience REM phases in their sleep, and it seems reasonable to suppose that other forms of life are subject to the same cycle of activity. However, so far no measurable proof of this has been available. REM phases undoubtedly regulate functions which are important to the life of the organism, and although their origin remains obscure, it is very probably closely related with the development of life.

Organic life on our planet has evolved by stages over thousands of millions of years. Its origin was not due to any unique combination of chance, but arose from inorganic matter as soon as the conditions were favourable to it. The origin of life was nothing more or less than a chemical reaction between different forms of matter, which arose inevitably from their molecular structure.

The American chemist and Nobel prize winner, Harold Clayton Urey (born 1893), was one of the first to suggest that the original atmosphere of the earth consisted of hydrogen compounds – at first without free hydrogen – unlike the oxygen-rich atmosphere which we have now. In this primeval atmosphere the necessary ingredients for the synthesis 'of organic structures – such as carbon in methane, oxygen in water, nitrogen in ammonia, hydrogen in hydrogen gas, and other gases – would already have been present.

In 1950 Urey's pupil Stanley Miller created a sensation by proving this theory in an experiment. Miller simulated the 'primeval atmosphere' in a system of closed glass retorts and tubes. What he did was to provide this system, by means of a container of boiling water, with a constant supply of steam, which was compounded with ammonia, hydrogen and methane. In another part of the system, Miller bombarded the mixture with high-frequency sparks, then led the condensed vapour back to the water container, where it was reheated. Within a few days, the water had turned pink, and after a week it was dark red. The results were sensational – 15 per cent of the carbon present in the methane had produced organic compounds, including amino-acids, which are the building blocks of all forms of animal and vegetable protein. Thus Miller had proved that the formation of organic structures of this kind was possible in a predominantly hydrogen environment.

In the early stages of the earth's existence, fundamental chemical changes took place in the planet's crust. Probably, the primeval seas and atmospheric gases were created by the formation of chemical compounds of carbon, methane, ammonia, hydrogen sulphide, water vapour and other gases. Scientists assume that carbon was present from the beginning in the form of hydrocarbons. This meant that innumerable chemical changes were possible, which could lead to the development of organic structures through reactions with the primeval atmosphere.

In this way a kind of primeval 'soup' was created which contained not only the raw material of life, but also the energy required for further chemical changes. The organic molecules combined in fairly simple formations, which separated into independent molecular systems in the form of tiny drops.

Some 3000 to 4000 million years ago, complex structures finally developed. The first basic cells were created. And since they were in the primeval ocean – a solution of hundreds of multifarious organic compounds and inorganic salts – they absorbed some of these substances in periodic phases of activity, and 'digested' them. The first primitive step towards 'metabolism' had been taken. These periodic – we would now say biorhythmic – phases of activity probably lie at the origin of the highly complex cycle of REM phases in humans and mammals.

The most important, and the most remarkable, step in the creation of life was the separation of the primitive cells from their environment. The cells now had to learn to differentiate between themselves and their surroundings. They were forced to cut themselves off. Membranes formed to enable them to do this, and they became individuals. The fight for existence, for survival, had begun.

The next milestone in the evolution of life lies some 1500 million years back. Suddenly, individual cells joined to form multiple cells. Possible mutations were the cause of these first 'malformations' from which man was eventually to develop.

Probably the first living molecules rapidly used up the available stock of natural organic matter, and perished as a result. But at this point in time some of the organisms which were being created began to produce new foodstuffs by means of photosynthesis and put life back on a stable footing. In the process of photosynthesis, primitive organisms use the energy which they absorb from light to extract organic food from inorganic substances.

Photosynthesis probably began on earth about 3400 million years ago, if we are to accept the evidence of fossils found in the oldest strata of sedimentary rock in the

Onverwacht strata in the South African Barberton highlands. Three NASA scientists, Dr Keith Kvenvolden, Dr William Schöpf and Dorothy Z. Oehler, are convinced that in this rock formation they have found evidence that the transition from primary to organic carbon is produced by photosynthetic organisms. As carbon is the basis of all terrestrial life, the carbon present in fossils forms a record of the appearance of life in its earliest stages.

Biorhythms were already present in the primitive cell with its periodic phases of activity. Photosynthesis marked the beginning of a new and more important cycle – that of light and dark, warm and cold. Photosynthesis released the vital oxygen which was changed into ozone by the ultra-violet rays of the sun. In this way an ozone layer slowly formed in the upper atmosphere, which protected life from the dangerous ultra-violet rays. The situation was quite the contrary to that in the early phase of organic life, in which these rays played a contributory role.

For a long time it remained a puzzle why evolution stuck at the single-cell stage for thousands of years, only to take a sudden jump to the stage of multiple cells, which assumed ever higher and more complex forms. Mutation was one explanation. Another, amazingly simple one was put forward by Steven M. Stanley, who holds the chair of palaeobiology at Johns Hopkins University in the United States.

Stanley's theory is based on the biological theory of 'cropping'. He uses the analogy of a lawn. If we are lucky, mainly grass will grow there under the right conditions. If we neglect the lawn, however, and let sheep and goats graze on it instead of mowing it, it will rapidly become overgrown with weeds. This is because the animals tend to tear the grass out in clumps, including the stalk and roots. Where there was once a well-kept lawn with one single plant species – grass – there will soon be a patchwork of weeds of all kinds.

If we apply Stanley's cropping theory to the Precambrian

era, some 2500 million years ago, it would mean that algae
and bacteria, for example, extracted their food from light and
the primeval soup, leaving no room for other types of life.
From this point evolution needed thousands of millions of
years before room could be made for higher life forms to
survive in a hostile environment.

Stanley takes the view that the limited character of the
whole terrestrial life system changed when this stage was
reached. Now animal-like organisms fed on algae and space
was created for other life-forms; with the appearance of richer
and more varied forms of food, new species began continually
developing. Evolution was in full swing. In order to survive,
multiple-celled organisms naturally had to meet far more
exacting requirements than single-celled organisms. Multiple-celled organisms had to be able to coordinate; for this
they required more energy, and this meant more food, which
in turn meant that they were exposed to greater danger. So
bundles of nerve cells were developed to coordinate the
working of the cells, and nerve connections to transmit
controlling impulses to the groups of cells. These nerve cells
were the starting point for the formation of the human brain,
eventually forming the lowest (anatomically) and the oldest
part, the brain stem. It is this area which controls the
important function of metabolism and the organism's cycle of
rest and activity.

The biorhythmic cycle – precursor of the later REM
phases – continued to fulfil purely physiological requirements even after the formation of the brain stem. It was
not until about 1000 million years ago, as multiple-celled
organisms became increasingly complex and the
diencephalon developed, that the transformation of the
biorhythmic phases of activity into REM phases began. For
in the diencephalon, which is common to man and the higher

animals, instinctive modes of behaviour are stored as in an archive. Inherited behaviour patterns, millions of years old, are stored here in man as in other animals, unconsciously influencing our thoughts and our actions. And newly acquired patterns began to be processed and stored in this part of the brain from that time on.

Opinions are still divided about the next gigantic step in the evolution of the brain – the leap from animal to man – despite the obvious attractions of Darwin and his theory of evolution by natural selection. Charles Darwin (1809–1882), who is erroneously thought to have maintained that man is descended from the apes, put forward the theory that every living being has a natural tendency to produce small bodily alterations. The struggle for survival in itself imposes a degree of selection which may have no significance in a higher evolutionary sense. By force of circumstance, forms of life which are better adapted to their environment have a greater capacity for survival, and will inevitably outlast the weaker forms.

Thus according to Darwin our so-called higher development is the inevitable consequence of a process of natural selection. But it was the natural philosopher and zoologist Ernst Haeckel (1834–1919), a passionate defender of the Darwinian doctrine of the origins of man, who was the first to see the evolutionary process as a single major growth. It was he who created a new branch of knowledge – phylogeny or the history of species – and drew a sharp distinction between this and ontogeny or the history of the development of the individual.

Haeckel sought out the vanished traces of our ancestors and reconstructed our lineage through its biogenetic principles. Following the mathematically exact formulae of genetics, he demonstrated that in the period between the first cell division and birth, an embryo cell in the mother's body undergoes all the stages of evolution in rapid succession.

From this fact, Haeckel was able to deduce the general pattern of human development from the Precambrian era to the present day.

Consider the words 'I love Lucy' – a notably macabre caption for a picture of a battered skull with empty eye sockets. Its fortunate discoverer holds it gingerly between his fingertips, eyeing it with an expression of mingled affection and distrust. And who would not, when suddenly faced with such a relic of his ancestors from the depths of prehistory?

Who is Lucy?

Lucy is the 3-million-year-old skeleton of a young woman, excavated by the American anthropologist Donald C. Johanson in the Ethiopian region of Afar. After he had painstakingly assembled the individual bones of his discovery, Johanson found that the woman had been over 1 metre in height, died at the age of twenty, could already walk upright and had shorter arms than the present-day anthropoid ape. He christened the 3-million-year-old figure Lucy.

But Lucy is not the only recent find to have raised a whole series of hypotheses about the point at which ape became man. In later excavations at the site where he had already found Lucy, Johanson found 150 more old bones from a number of adults and two children. These had probably perished in a flood catastrophe $3\frac{1}{2}$ million years ago – half a million years earlier than Lucy.

Among the same range of relics we must include the 2.6-million-year-old humanoid skull found by anthropologist Richard Leakey under volcanic rock strata in northern Kenya. This small skull, now registered under its find number, ER 1470, had a brain capacity of 800 ml – already a substantial capacity in comparison with the 1500 ml of modern man.

Finds such as these, and the fossils from increasingly further removed epochs which have recently been coming to light, make the problem of establishing the point at which the transition from animal to man took place increasingly difficult and complex. In 1975 Dr F. C. Howell of California University called for the abandonment of a whole series of old hypotheses and suggested that it would be better to start again from the beginning.

Johanson and Leakey concluded from the bones which they discovered that after the transition from animal to man towards the end of the Tertiary period a whole series of two-legged beings developed who could work stone in an intelligent fashion. The so-called large-brained bipeds probably became engaged in a struggle for survival with the ape-man who later became extinct at a far earlier period than was previously supposed. They can be considered our own ancestors, or at least their relatives.

The skull found by Leakey with its appreciable brain capacity was adduced as evidence for this theory, for it differs considerably from others from the same epoch.

Anthropologists now suspect that the division of *Homo* from the family of hominids took place as early as 4 to 6 million years ago; however, researchers have yet to find the skeletal remains from this period which would confirm this theory.

One of the most interesting deductions which Johanson and Leakey made from their finds was that our 'ancestors' were by no means 'killer apes', but on the contrary beings who lived in social groups unlike any other animal. The much-aired view that man is burdened with inherited aggressions perhaps needs some revision in the light of this view.

Some 500 million years ago, then, the formation of the cerebrum marked the most portentous event in evolution – the origins of consciousness. The distinguished Australian neurophysiologist John C. Eccles, who was awarded the Nobel Prize in 1963, comments: 'For each of us our brain embodies the foundation of our personal identity, which is revealed through our own ego and our character, i.e.

it characterizes the essential *I* in each of us. It gives each of us experiences and memories, ideas and dreams.'

It seems likely that dreaming – or the REM phases of sleep – played a significant part in the formation of the cerebrum. Eccles and other scientists have recently shown that new experiential stimuli lead to changes in the brain, resulting in the formation of new synapses or nerve-structures. The electro-biochemical processes of REM sleep in which new experiential data are processed and programmed must therefore have played an important role in the evolution of consciousness.

As early as 1780, the Italian anatomist Michele Gaetano Malacarne proved that experience produces changes in the brain, in an experiment using pairs of animals from the same brood or litter. He took two dogs, two goldfinches and two blackbirds and trained one of each pair over a long period, leaving the others untrained as a control. Later he killed all the animals and dissected their brains. He found that the cerebellums of the trained animals were visibly more corrugated than those of the untrained animals.

Malacarne's contemporaries showed little interest in this discovery, and only a few years ago some American researchers surprised the scientific world with similar results. L. Benett, Director of the Lawrence-Berkeley Laboratory for Chemical Biodynamics, Miriam Cleeves, a professor of psychology, and Mark R. Rosenzweig, a professor of psychology, found that the brains of rats showed unmistakable anatomical and chemical changes after only a month of exposure to specific experiences. We cannot say specifically why and how evolution took place, for we are not in the position of objective observers watching the process from its beginnings. We are in fact just *one* product of the evolutionary process and, as *Homo sapiens,* probably not even its end product. For evolution continues – and will do so as long as man refrains from bringing himself to a premature and violent end.

Undoubtedly both natural selection and the absorption of new and significant experiential data – which run completely counter to inherited, instinctive behaviour patterns – have played an important role in the development of man. The result, in any case, is a mere 1–1½ kg of white and pinkish-grey matter with a phenomenal output.

The cortex or outer grey matter of the brain, about 3 mm thick and containing over 10,000 million nerve cells, is the centre of human reason and unreason. Large parts of this outer layer are completely 'empty', i.e. there are no behaviour patterns 'imprinted' on them. Thus they are available to deal with the constantly changing impressions and experiential data which stream in from our environment – they are our reserve.

Let us imagine that it were possible to build a computer with the capacity of the human brain, one which could think creatively and abstractly, and was able to dream as well. Such an apparatus would probably be larger than the Empire State Building, and its cost would undoubtedly ruin any existing nation on this earth. It has been estimated that the cost of such an enterprise would be in the region of one trillion pounds sterling – a million to the power of three. Its energy consumption would be equivalent to that of a medium-sized town. And in any case, in order to build and program this giant computer, we would still need our 1–1½ kg of white and pinkish grey matter, which can do the job so much better in the first place. A super-computer of this order would have to have an enormous and flexible memory – a kind of dynamic data bank – in order to simulate the human memory. The main feature of our memory is its flexibility – it is not a rigid mechanism, it works creatively and selectively, as is most clearly demonstrated by our dreams both by day and at night.

But what is memory?

Until quite recently, scientists were generally convinced

that this could never be answered, but now that view has changed dramatically. Some remarkable experiments have been conducted in this field, and brain researchers have been able to isolate the so-called memory substance in the brain. Some notable work has been done by Professor George Ungar of Houston University.

As has so often been the case in science some of the most important evidence has been produced by experiments with animals. The breakthrough can be traced to the first, highly controversial experiments with planarians, or flatworms, conducted by the American professor James McConnell. He was particularly interested in flatworms because of their amazing tenacity. They are practically impossible to kill, since if they are cut into two or four, the parts turn into complete individual worms. McConnell wanted to know whether the sectioned worms which have grown a new head or tail shared the experiences of the original worm, or whether each portion had to start collecting new experiences.

This basic question underlay all McConnell's experiments. He took a number of flatworms and put them in a basin of water, then subjected them to low-tension electrical shocks accompanied by a green signal light, which made the worms curl up in pain. After repeating this treatment for some time, he started flashing the green light by itself, without administering the electrical shock. The worms still curled up; they had learned to associate the green light with pain and reacted accordingly.

Next, McConnell separated the flatworms' heads from their tails and waited until a new tail had been formed. Then he exposed the old heads with their new bodies to the same flashing light as he had the original worms, and remarkably enough these worms also curled up, even though they had received no electric shock. To complete the experiment, McConnell now took the original bodies which had grown new heads and subjected them to the same treatment. He merely wished to establish that nothing would happen – after all the new heads did not have the information imparted by the training process. But to his amazement, he found that these worms also reacted by rolling up when the green signal light was flashed. The information had somehow been transferred into the new heads, but how? McConnell decided to experiment further. He cut up some of his trained worms into tiny pieces and fed them to untrained worms to eat. The untrained worms digested both their companions and the knowledge stored in them. When the green light was flashed they too rolled up in expectation of an electric shock.

McConnell seemed to have proved that knowledge was an edible commodity. But unexpectedly, perhaps, when he first aired this view in public he got little but derision from his colleagues, and comments such as 'Have a professor for breakfast' seemed to express the general view. But today, scarcely fifteen years later, brain researchers have fundamentally changed their views. Many of those who started by ridiculing McConnell's experiments now recognize his contribution to the field of brain research.

But that was only the beginning. Since then Professor Richard Gray of the University of Western Michigan has proved that knowledge can be administered by injection. He was the first man to induce a fear of dark holes in rats. We all know that rats will instinctively hide in dark holes and corners, and Gray made use of this in his experiments. The rats he used as subjects were given the choice of crawling along a runway into a dark cage or a light one. Naturally they ran instinctively into the dark one, but as soon as they did so a trap door closed behind them and they were subjected to electric shocks for several seconds. After five days of this treatment the rats had learned their lesson. Nothing would induce them to go into the dark cages.

Gray now killed the trained rats, processed their brains into a solution and injected other, untrained rats with the mixture. The results exceeded all his expectations, for the dead rats' fear of the dark was transferred to the living, untrained rats with the injection. In further experiments, the untrained animals stopped, trembling at the entrance to the darkened cages.

Experiments now followed one another in quick succession. Other research laboratories carried out similar tests on other animals. All had the same object – to prove that experience can be transmitted by means of injections – and the results were generally affirmative.

For a long time scientists believed that memory – which naturally includes our acquired experiences – is stored in the electrical currents of the brain. But as a result of all these experiments on animals it became clear that the substance of our knowledge is not electrical, but something far more tangible – namely biochemical – in nature. It had been proved that knowledge could be injected; it now remained to isolate from the suspension of brain matter the actual substance which forms the stuff of our thoughts.

The man who had the courage to embark on the search for the molecule of knowledge was the American pharmacologist Professor George Ungar of Baylor College of Medicine at Houston University in Texas. Ungar started from the assumption that the memory substance would be present only in minuscule traces, visible only under the electron microscope. Evidently he would only be able to discover it if he had a substantial supply of trained brain matter on which to experiment.

Ungar now embarked on a mammoth undertaking. He trained tens of thousands of fish to avoid blue or green lights. A similar quantity had to learn to swim on their backs, although a cork waistcoat fixed to their bellies made this extremely difficult. Hordes of rats were made afraid of the dark. As soon as the behaviour pattern had been learned, the animals were killed and put on ice until there was a large enough quantity of trained brain matter available for the search to begin. Finally everything was ready. Ten pounds of rat brains at a time were reduced to a broth and, with the help of sieves, centrifuges and filters, Ungar attempted to isolate the memory substance. One component of the mixture after another was filtered out and tested on animals to see if the memory substance was still there. From ten pounds of rat brains, all that finally remained was the unimaginably small quantity of 1.5 thousandths of a gram of a homogenous substance. Ungar called this 'scotophobin' (from the Greek *scotophobia* = fear of the dark) because it was the medium which had recorded fear of the dark in rats.

When scotophobin was analysed, it turned out to be a protein-like substance, the individual molecules of which each consisted of a chain of fifteen amino-acids. External impressions – i.e. information – cause a 'matrix' to be produced in the nucleus of a nerve cell, 'imprints' of which are linked to a protein molecule in the ribosomes (protein particles containing ribonucleic acid). These are then stored in the cell as the memory substance.

Only a few months after Ungar's discovery, the German biochemist Wolfgang Parr succeeded in producing a few micrograms of artificial scotophobin. He got in touch with Ungar, and the latter injected his rats with the artificial substance to such good effect that they fled in panic from dark holes after being injected.

But scotophobin is not the only memory molecule; in the meantime Ungar had isolated another from the brains of 6000 rats which he had trained to react to a shrill bell. This memory molecule was christened amelin, and it consisted of six amino-acids. Ungar's work is by no means at an end. He is already looking for new memory molecules and even intends to test them on human beings, with himself as the initial subject.

Work is also being done on the synthetic production of

other memory molecules. However outlandish it may sound, there seems no doubt that sooner or later we will be able to acquire synthetically produced knowledge, by taking injections of the appropriate substance. Perhaps one day we will even be able to buy synthetic dream capsules from the chemist to colour our nightly REM periods. The possibilities are endless.

9

The Ivory Gate

For the Greek poet Homer there were two sorts of dreams – the real ones which come through the ivory gate, and the false ones which creep in through the gate of horn. They are dreams from different hemispheres.

Our brain has two hemispheres, the left and the right, each of which fulfils a specific function. The left hemisphere of the cerebrum is responsible for everything practical – our speech, bodily functions, rational and intellectual thought. The right hemisphere by contrast is the creative and abstract one. It is responsible for artistic activity, for our intuitions and emotions, for our capacity for imagination and dreaming.

Professor Roger Sperry of the California Institute of Technology demonstrated on epileptics that each of these brain hemispheres operates independently of the other. He also showed that the right- and left-hand functioning of the cerebrum have an effect on our dreams.

A hundred years ago surgeons already knew that speech is affected if the left half of the brain is damaged, while damage to the right hemisphere affects spatial perception. Professor Sperry and his colleagues were able to collect a great deal of useful data on the functioning of the human brain from epileptics whose hemispheres had been surgically separated as a means of controlling epileptic seizures. The bundles of nerve fibre which join the two hemispheres of the cerebrum were cut through, with the result that, as Sperry said, 'what is experienced in the right hemisphere seems to be completely outside the awareness of the left'.

During the course of Sperry's research, it often appeared that the left half of the brain was unaware of what the right was doing. For example, one patient was blindfolded and given a familiar object to hold – a fork. The patient was able to demonstrate with gestures what it was, but was quite unable to say the word fork. He could even pick a fork out blindfold from a pile of other objects, but the word fork never passed his lips.

The subject was then made to reach for the fork with his right hand – still with his eyes covered – so that the left hemisphere was forced into operation. He could now pronounce the word fork at his first attempt.

Sperry concluded that under such circumstances as these, the functions of the two halves of the brain can overlap one another. Also the left hemisphere did not seem entirely to trust its partner. One of Sperry's patients and his wife always referred to what they called 'that sneaky left hand'. Often the wife would aggressively push that hand away, preferring to invoke the aid of the right hand – or more exactly of the left hemisphere. Obviously the two halves of the brain had come into conflict with one another. The right hemisphere showed a remarkable talent for mastering manual tasks, but was quite incompetent at any form of calculation, being unable even to add four and four.

In healthy people, the two halves of the brain naturally cooperate, even if one or the other is more or less dominant. This phenomenon also explains the different capabilities and talents to be found in different people, and the different personalities which they express. According to one theory, the hemispheres of the cerebrum carry out an 'emergency drill' from time to time during REM sleep –i.e. they prepare themselves for an eventuality in which the brain, say, is damaged, and one hemisphere has to intervene in the field of operation of the other. Analysis of our dreams shows that in non-REM dreams the left half of the brain is dominant, while in REM dreams the right half is dominant.

Calvin Hall, Professor of Psychology and Director of the Institute of Dream Research at Santa Cruz, is interested in the problem of dream interpretation primarily from a scientific standpoint. He found the dream theories put forward by the psychoanalysts in the 1940s increasingly unsatisfactory, primarily because they were based on atypical dream material provided by patients.

Hall wanted to know what the so-called normal man dreamed about, not the psychically disturbed individual, and he instituted a research programme to this end. During the course of the project, which involved decades of work by himself and his colleagues, dream material from people in many countries and strata of society was gathered together and analysed. In his book *The Individual and his Dreams*, Hall writes:

> During the past twenty-five years we have read and analysed thousands of dreams. We are familiar with the dreams of Australian aborigines, Zulus, Nigerians, Navaho and Hopi Indians, Mexicans, Peruvians, Argentineans, American Negroes, and many other national and ethnic groups. We have analysed dreams reported by climbers on the American Mount Everest expedition, dream diaries of a child molester and a blind man, and dreams of homosexuals, alcoholics, schizophrenics, transvestites, patients undergoing psychoanalysis, schoolchildren, college students, and people sleeping under laboratory conditions.

We have read dream series published by prominent
people, those of Freud and Jung, Franz Kafka, Julian
Green, William Dean Howells, Eugene Ionesco, Robert
Lowie, Jack Kerouac, and Howard Nemerov. We have
also read and analysed dream diaries of more ordinary
people: an Ohio factory worker, a British professor, a
California secretary, a Santa Cruz surfer, a New England
physiologist, a Pennsylvania schoolteacher, a Swiss
chemist, a woman psychologist, a New York businessman,
an Israeli official, a San Francisco writer, a Texas
engineer, a Los Angeles high-school student, and many
others.

Our collection contains over 50,000 dreams gathered
from all over the world.

This material led Hall to the conclusion that most dreams
are entirely prosaic in nature. Buildings and people appear,
mostly members of the dreamer's family or close friends.
Thirty per cent of all dream activities are familiar bodily
movements such as walking, jumping, riding, etc. Passive
activities such as sitting, watching, talking, etc. make up 50
per cent of the dream content. Women's dreams are usually
more passive than those of men.

Hall's investigation also revealed that people have far more
unpleasant dreams than they do pleasant ones. And the bad
dreams become more frequent with increasing age. Fear is
more common in dreams than anger, and happiness is far
rarer than sadness. On the other hand, erotic elements
appear in 50 per cent of all dreams. Hall suggests that the
figure could be even higher, since erotic dreams could well
have been suppressed by the subjects more often than other
varieties. We practically never dream about our place of
work – the office, the factory, etc. Hall takes the view that the
absence of such dreams is basically due to our aversion to
work, learning and business in general. Understandably, we

would much rather spend our time following our own preferences. The main fabric of our dreams in fact is derived from the world of our feelings, from our intimate, personal life and our private conflicts.

For Hall, dreams are quite simply the natural pictorial language of the sleeper. Thoughts are transformed into pictures by which the dreamer can be neither deliberately deceived nor led astray.

'A dream is a personal document, a letter to oneself,' says Hall.

He found absolutely no confirmation of the Freudian theory that in dreaming our unfulfilled sexual needs are censored and appear only in a masked form, lest our delicate conscience should be offended and we should wake up in fright. Hall established that on the contrary a dreamer can have a symbolic sexual dream one night and an unmistakably non-symbolic one the next night. Why should the dreaming brain bother with a deliberate masquerade one night, Hall asks, only to throw it recklessly aside the next? The incredible number of sexual symbols alone makes nonsense of the psychoanalytical theory of disguise. In a survey of specialist literature, Hall discovered 102 dream symbols for the penis and ninety-five for the vagina.

> If all these are merely masks for forbidden sexual thoughts, dream interpretation is reduced to a boring discovery that we are all sex-obsessed, which even if true would scarcely be very helpful.

writes Dr Ann Faraday in *Dream Power*. Dr Faraday wholeheartedly supports Hall's criticisms of Freudian dream interpretation, a technique which is still in use today.

Hall not only analysed the dreams of Mr Average, he even tackled the high priests of dream interpretation. He examined the dreams of Sigmund Freud and C. G. Jung and came to some surprising conclusions.

Freud's dreams turned out to contain more people than those of Jung. This coincides with observations on the two men's degree of sociability in everyday life. Freud liked company and had many friends and acquaintances; Jung on the other hand was a lone wolf. He preferred to withdraw into monastic seclusion and enjoy nature. His sociability was confined to his family, and the fact that many members of his family appeared in his dreams seems to confirm this.

Both men were equally open in their dreams, but whereas Jung in his dreams always appeared friendly and ready to make the first approach, in Freud's dreams it was always someone else who took the first step. It is often said of Freud that he expected everyone to come to him. Once, when he was staying in Switzerland, he was deeply offended that Jung had not felt it necessary to visit him.

Unlike Jung, Freud often dreamed of food and other forms of consumption. In his daily life Freud consumed an enormous number of thick cigars. He also lived in constant fear of becoming dependent on others. Freud himself said that people are usually most afraid of the thing which they really want the most, and according to this hypothesis, his fear of becoming dependent was in reality a reaction against subconscious desire to be looked after. This unconscious wish has its origin in the oral phase of babyhood, when the infant is dependent on the mother. A large proportion of Freud's dreams were oral in character, reflecting the childish longing hidden beneath the fear of the adult.

The attitude towards the sexes displayed by Freud and Jung in their dreams is interesting, for there was a distinct difference between the two. A normal man more often has arguments with men in his dreams, while his relationships with women are more often friendly. Jung's dreams were normal in this respect, but Freud's were quite the contrary. He often had quarrels with women, while his relationships with men were basically friendly. Freud had close friendships with a number of men. He talked of overcoming his homosexuality and admitted having a love-hate relationship with men. Freud once wrote to a colleague that the affection of a spirited and understanding group of young men was the most precious thing which psychoanalysis had given him.

Hall concludes that Freud suffered from an inverted Oedipus complex which impressed its mark on his personality and his dreams, and adduces the evidence of Freud's own words and those of his biographer, as well as the dreams themselves. In his analysis of Jung, he observes that there was nothing in the latter's life apart from the typical male Oedipus complex.

The psychotherapist Paul J. Stern has published a study entitled *C.G. Jung – The Haunted Prophet*, (New York: George Braziller, 1976), in which he states that half-way through his life Jung reached the borders of psychosis, and his work is the result of his neuroses. Although he was able to save himself from insanity, Stern considers, the schizophrenic distortion of his personality was irreparable. The parable of the mote and the beam springs irresistibly to mind.

Dream research is one of the most popular scientific specialities in America today. Over 500 psychoanalysts, physiologists and neurologists are working on dream-research projects. Among them is Rosalind Cartwright, a psychologist at Illinois University, who has drawn the following conclusions from more than 2000 recorded dreams:

Men are frequently involved in fighting in dreams, and often see themselves naked. Their favourite dream subjects are cars, travel and money. They are more active in their dreams than women. The latter often dream that they are being pursued by a stranger, and like flying in their dreams.

The content of dreams is the result of the civilization in which they occur, for they reflect the cultural influences of their time. Comparative studies between rural and urban children, for example, show that the events in their dreams reflect their surroundings. But in the final analysis, as an old Chinese proverb says, 'falcons and dreams are what one makes of them'.

In eighteenth-century China a good-looking youth named Pao Yu dreamed of a garden which was absolutely identical with that of his home. He was amazed that a garden could be so exactly like his own. A pair of servant girls came up to him, and Pao Yu was speechless. He could not understand how someone else's servants could look so exactly like Hsi Yen, Pin Ehr and all the other girls who worked for his parents.

Pao You thought the girls had recognized him. He went up to them and said: 'I'm just going for a walk. Do you want to come with me?'

The servant girls looked at him and burst out laughing.

'We must have been blind,' they said. 'How could we possibly confuse you with our master Pao Yu? He's so much nicer than you are.'

They were the servants of another Pao Yu.

'But I am Pao Yu,' our hero protested. 'Who is your master?'

'Pao Yu,' they answered. 'That was the name his parents gave him. Pao means Precious and Yu means Jade. May he have long life and happiness. How dare you usurp his name?'

When Pao Yu heard these words he couldn't believe his ears. No one had ever spoken to him like that before. Could there really be another Pao Yu?

'I must find out what's behind this,' he thought.

While he was pondering the matter he suddenly found himself back in a garden which seemed strangely familiar. He went up the steps and entered a room. There he saw a young man lying on a bed. Some girls were busy nearby, laughing amongst themselves. One of them said to the young man: 'What were you dreaming about, Pao Yu? Why do you look so sad?'

'I dreamed I was in a garden,' the youth replied, 'and none of you recognized me. You took no notice of me. I followed you home and found another Pao Yu sleeping in my bed.'

When Pao Yu heard this conversation he could not contain himself, and burst out:

'I'm looking for someone called Pao Yu – you must be him!'

The young man rose from his bed, embraced him and called out:

'It wasn't a dream, then. You are Pao Yu.'

Out in the garden someone called: 'Pao Yu.'

Both Pao Yus were stricken with fear. The Pao Yu of the dream disappeared, and the other called after him:

'Come again soon, Pao Yu.'

Pao Yu woke up, and his servant girls asked him:

'What were you dreaming about, Pao Yu. Why do you look so sad?'

'I had the strangest dream,' answered Pao Yu. 'I dreamed I was in a garden and none of you recognized me . . .'

The Chinese have long maintained two contradictory attitudes towards dreams. The traditional view sees dreaming as a motivating force, regarding it as an unequivocal pointer to existing aspects of reality. The other view mistrusts dream images, regarding them as deceptive phenomena whose causes need to be investigated by analytical methods.

Interestingly enough it is precisely these two contradictory attitudes towards dreaming which characterize the two main schools of psychoanalysis today – the mystical and the rationalist, the ivory gate and the gate of horn, Jung and Freud. According to the old Chinese saying, dreams are what we make of them. But what is perhaps more interesting is what they make of us.

Dreams and visions have always had a significant influence on the course of human history. It hardly matters whether the great historical dreams are authentic or not. The real

measure of their importance is their effect on the origins of
world religions and beliefs. The niceties of historical detail
can be left to the historians. It is the beliefs of nations and
populations which have shaped history.

One such belief is that enshrined in the religion of
Buddhism, which had its origin on a moonlit night in May,
some 2500 years ago.

Prince Siddhartha was thirty-five years old and had made
himself a bed of straw for the night. As he lay there, Mara, the
evil one, attacked him with the powers of darkness, and tried
to overcome him with fire and force. But his arts were of no
avail and he withdrew. The moon rode high in the sky as the
prince sank deep in meditation, as he had done a thousand
times before. Victory was near as he reached the goal of
hundreds of previous lifetimes of effort, devoted to a single
end. Looking back, he experienced his earlier births, the
cause of each rebirth and the suffering which followed. The
illumination which he had so long struggled for was now his.
He recognized that desire brings suffering, that when desire is
overcome, suffering too is at an end. It was here that the
journey ended.

The new Buddha was born about 520 years before Christ.
Buddha's enlightenment – his dream – was the kernel and
the original cause of Buddhism, which eventually became the
religion of the greater part of Asia. Buddha came from the
noble family of the Sakyas, who were natives of the foothills of
the Nepalese Himalayas. Prince Suddhodana, his father,
lived in the state capital of Kapilavastu, and his mother,
Maya, gave birth to him on a journey to the nearby Lumbini
Gardens. This was the place where she had once fallen asleep
and had a dream which she related to the prince and his
retinue, asking for an interpretation.

'Silver white and brighter than the sun – more beautiful
than the stately elephant on balanced joints and with six tusks
as hard as stone, the Enlightened One filled my body.'

And the brahmans answered her:

'Overwhelming happiness is foretold. This bodes no ill for the dynasty. Maya will bear a son. The offspring of royal blood, he will achieve universal power. But he will leave his capital and his princedom against his family's wishes. Filled with compassion for the three worlds, he will become a wandering monk, cut off from everything. He will strive for good in all three worlds, and bring peace.'

It is related that Prince Suddhodana tried by all means to withhold the knowledge of earthly suffering from his son. But one day, as the young prince Siddhartha was leaving the palace in his hunting carriage, he saw an old man, then a sick man, and finally a corpse. Each time he asked the coachman what this meant.

'We all have to come to this,' the coachman replied.

The prince was deeply disturbed, for now he saw clearly the consequences of birth.

Later, he saw a shaven-headed hermit in a tattered yellow robe. When he asked the coachman who this was, he replied: 'One who has left house and home and given up all worldly goods.'

The prince returned to the palace deep in thought and decided to renounce all worldly pleasures. That night he came to the decision to release not only himself but the whole world from the suffering of birth. . . He took leave of his sleeping wife and child, and left the palace in the silence of the Indian night to become a wandering monk.

According to Buddhist belief a Buddha will appear again some time in the future, for in the Indian view of history there are no single historical events, only cyclic repetitions, continuing for all eternity.

In the Christian Bible there are some seventy passages relating to dreams and visions. In the New Testament we are told that the coming of Christ was announced to Mary in a dream. She dreamed of the event at night, while Joseph

dreamed of it in the daytime. The three wise men from the
East, too, were inspired by a dream to set out for Bethlehem.
Strangely, not a single dream of Christ's is related in the
Bible. Both Buddha and Muhammad, on the other hand, are
traditionally supposed to have dreamed.

The Archangel Gabriel appeared to Muhammad in a
dream when he was sleeping between the hills of Safa and
Meeva. He was leading the grey mare Elboraq and ordered
Muhammad to get up and accompany him on a long journey.
In a flash the silver-white horse brought him first to
Jerusalem. There he met Abraham, Moses and Jesus and
they prayed together in the temple. Then Gabriel took him
flying through the seven heavenly spheres, shining in all the
colours of the rainbow. He was taken before Adam, Enoch,
Aaron, Moses and Abraham, one after the other, and they all
greeted him as the greatest of all prophets. Finally, Muhammad rode on Elboraq's back across the ocean of light to the
throne of the Almighty. God ordered him to say fifty prayers
each day, but yielded before Muhammad's entreaties, reduc-
ing the number to five. Finally, Elboraq took him back to the
place where he had gone to sleep many hours beforehand.

Islam, the religion of which Muhammad (AD 570–630) is
the prophet, was founded in Mecca and Medina between 610
and 632. Following the inspiration of Muhammad's dream, it
became the newest of the world's religions, and today has
about 460 million adherents.

Abdullah ben Zaid, one of Mohammed's followers, fell
asleep while he was praying and dreamed of a man in green
clothing who held a rattle in his hand. He asked the green
man to give him the rattle, so that he could use it to call
people to prayer, and the green man answered: 'Call out:
there is no god but God, and Muhammad is his prophet.'

When he woke up, Abdullah ben Zaid immediately related
his dream to Muhammad and his followers and the prophet
asked him to teach the call, word for word, to the priest Bilal

the Ethiopian. Thus it was that Bilal became the first *muezzin*, and now, five times a day, the *muezzin* sings the *adhan*, calling the faithful to prayer.

There are fewer surviving accounts of political dreams than there are of religious ones, and perhaps understandably. After the statesmen of ancient times, there were few politicians prepared to admit that their dubious activities had been inspired by dreams.

As the Roman writer Valerius Maximus (*circa* AD 31) related, the famous Carthaginian general Hannibal (247–183 BC) harboured a burning hatred for the Roman Empire. So he was all the more pleased when one day he had a dream full of frightful images which seemed to coincide exactly with his own intentions. In this dream a man appeared to Hannibal, as handsome as a young god, and declared that he had been sent by heaven to call upon him to invade Italy. When Hannibal looked around him he saw a gigantic snake cruelly and brutally destroying everything which stood in its way. Behind the reptile the heavens were darkened with clouds of smoke and torn by flashes of lightning. Thoroughly shaken by this vision, Hannibal asked the dream god what it meant.

The god answered: 'It is the collapse of Italy and all that lies in store for it – go, and fulfil its destiny.'

We need hardly recall the devastation which Hannibal wrought on his campaigns through Italy. The Romans' cry of terror – '*Hannibal ante portas*' – which greeted Hannibal's arrival at the gates of Rome in 211 BC is evidence enough. Hannibal fulfilled his dream – he accomplished the fate of Italy.

Some 2000 years after Hannibal, Prince Otto von Bismarck, Chancellor of the German Reich, wrote to Kaiser Wilhelm I on 18 December 1881:

Your Majesty's communication encourages me to relate a

dream which I had early in 1863, when the strife was at its worst and the human eye could see no way out. I dreamed, and related to my wife and other witnesses the next morning, that I was riding along a narrow alpine path with a precipice on the right and cliffs on the left. The path became so narrow that the horse refused to continue, but there was no room either to turn round or dismount. So I struck the sheer face of the rocks with the switch I held in my left hand and called upon God. The switch grew long, and the rock-face fell back like a piece of theatre scenery revealing a broad pathway with a view of hills and woodland as in Bohemia. Prussian troops appeared with banners and while still in the dream I wondered how I could bring the news to your Majesty as quickly as possible. This dream came true, and I woke from it full of joy and new strength.

In this dream Bismarck thought that he had foreseen the German victory in the struggle against Austria. Later, however, Sigmund Freud gave it a rather less prophetic interpretation, characteristically finding in it a purely sexual significance. He saw the switch as a symbol of the male member, signifying self-gratification and erotic conquest.

Another scene of war – the French front, 1917. Corporal Adolf Hitler started from his sleep in fright. He had dreamed that he was buried under melting ice and earth, his chest covered in blood, unable to breathe. He believed it to be a warning, though all was quiet on the section of the front which his Bavarian regiment was defending. Uneasily, he left his dug-out, climbed out of the trench and ran away from the lines. He must have been aware that he ran a far greater risk of being hit by a bullet outside the trench, but driven by some inner impulse he still ran. Suddenly he was thrown to the ground by the blast from a nearby explosion. An enemy shell had burst in his section of the front. A single shot, not more.

Now wide awake, Hitler ran back to the trench, but there was not a living soul to be seen. Everything had been laid flat. The entrance to the dug-out was blocked, his comrades buried under masses of earth.

From this day on, Hitler believed that he had a divine mission to fulfil.

These few dreams have been selected from innumerable accounts of religious and political dreams to show the enormous influence which a dream can have on the course of historical events. Very often, of course, dreams were dressed up and used for propaganda purposes. But whatever their real nature, the only true measure of their importance is their historical impact.

Both science and the arts have been inspired to a remarkable extent by dreams. Perhaps this is because the two hemispheres of the brain – those governing intuition and intellect – cooperate better in dreaming, enabling intuition to be expressed more clearly.

Albert Einstein (1879–1955) once wrote that there are no logical rules to help us to establish elementary laws. Only intuition is in a position to do this. The basis of this theory of relativity, for example, came to him when he was lying ill in bed.

The pioneer of chemical heavy industry, Friedrich August Kekulé von Stradonitz (1829–1896) made two of the most significant contributions to the theoretical bases of organic chemistry with his discovery of the tetravalence of carbon and the ring-shaped structure of the benzene molecule. He related how he made this discovery to a fascinated audience in the summer of 1890 in Berlin. The German Chemistry Society was celebrating the twenty-fifth anniversary of Kekulé's benzene theory and its inventor was giving a talk, not about chemical bonding but about a dream. Kekulé described how he had been sitting in his study in Ghent, unable to make any progress.

'I turned the chair towards the fire and sank into a doze. The atoms danced before my eyes. My mind's eye, sharpened by long familiarity with such visions, now distinguished larger formations of various different shapes. Long rows, many times more densely packed, all in movement, twisting and turning like snakes. And look, what was that? One of the snakes was biting its own tail, the image circled mockingly before my eyes. I woke up in a flash. And this time, too, I needed the rest of the night to work out the rest of the hypothesis.

'If we learn to dream, gentlemen, then perhaps we may find the truth.'

With these words Kekulé finished his address and went out, leaving a bewildered audience behind him.

The celebrated physicist Niels Bohr (1885–1962) struggled with his model of the atom for many years before his theory finally 'hatched out' in a dream in 1913. He saw himself sitting on a sun of flaring gas while planets whizzed by at breakneck speed. The surrounding planets seemed to be connected to the sun by slender threads. Suddenly the gas thickened, the sun and its planets shrank together and froze. Bohr related that at that moment he awoke and immediately realized that he had seen the model of the atom. In 1922, Niels Bohr received the Nobel Prize for the result of his dream.

The serologist and Nobel Prize-winner Paul Ehrlich (1854–1915) said that in a dream he saw clearly how cells defend themselves against poisons which penetrate the organism. This theory eventually led to the discovery of the arsenical compound salvarsan used to combat syphilis.

In 1960 the German-American physiologist Dr Otto Loewi described in the autumn number of the journal *Perspectives in Biology and Medicine* how he won the Nobel Prize as a result of a dream. The best known part of his scientific work, he wrote, was the theory of the chemical transmission of nervous impulses which he put forward in 1921. Until then it had generally been thought that the nervous impulse was transmitted directly from the nerve ending to the functioning organ by means of an electrical impulse.

Back in 1903 Leowi had discussed with a colleague the fact that certain drugs will have the effect of enhancing or dampening the reactions of the sympathetic or parasympathetic nervous system. This conversation suggested to Loewi that the nerve endings might contain chemical substances which are set free by stimulation of the nerves, and he wondered whether the chemical substances might not themselves transmit the nervous impulses to the organs. As at the time he did not have the facilities to prove it experimentally, he forgot the idea, until it came up again in 1920.

In the night before Easter Sunday he suddenly woke up, found a light, and made some notes on a scrap of paper. At six o'clock the next morning he remembered that he had written down something important during the night, but he was unable to decipher his scrawled notes.

The following night he was woken again around three o'clock by the same thought. It was a plan for an experiment which would prove or disprove the hypothesis of chemical transmission which he had discussed seventeen years earlier. Loewi immediately got up, went to his laboratory and carried out the experiment he had dreamed of on frogs's hearts. The results of this experiment formed the corner-stone of his theory of the chemical transmission of nervous impulses.

The field of literature contains many examples of dreams providing the motivating force for works by the great philosophers, poets and novelists. Italy's greatest poet, Dante (1265-1321) was inspired by dreams in producing his *Divina Commedia*. In this he related his visionary journey through the three stages of the beyond, while his *Vita nuova* tells of his mystical love for Beatrice.

The French philosopher and mathematician René

Descartes (1596–1650), author of the famous phrase, *Cogito ergo sum* (I think, therefore I am), also traced his most important philosophical insights to a series of dreams. But his main preoccupation was with the subjectivity of all sense perceptions.

Johann Wolfgang von Goethe (1749–1832) even used the dream as a literary technique in part two of *Faust*.

Robert Louis Stevenson (1850–1894) admitted that most of his themes were inspired by dreams. He described himself as 'a notable dreamer'. One of his works – *The Strange Case of Dr Jekyll and Mr Hyde* – is a fascinating account of a split personality.

Franz Kafka (1883–1924) also has to be mentioned here, for the works which he has left us are nothing more nor less than a series of nightmares, and must doubtless have been strongly influenced by his dreams. We need only think of the commercial traveller in *Metamorphosis* who wakes up one morning as a beetle and perishes at the hands of his unloving and uncomprehending relations. Or the execution machine of *In the Penal Settlement*, which etches the words of the sentence into the flesh of its victims.

Of the innumerable painters who have recorded their dreams in paint only a few, chosen more or less at random, can be mentioned. There are the grisly fantasies of Hieronymus Bosch, for example, representing the Last Judgement, the punishments of Hell, the mortal sins and the temptation of Adam and Eve. Or the impressive silence of Arnold Böcklin's island of the dead. Or the fairy-tale pictures of Marc Chagall, painted in glowing, dream-like colours. And innumerable Surrealist works by artists such as Salvador Dali, Joan Miró, Max Ernst, Matta, Enrico Donati or Yves Tanguy; by Paul Delvaux, Francis Picabia, Giorgio di Chirico and Henri Rousseau, whose artistic visions transform the very bases of our reality into quicksand.

The Italian writer Giovanni Papini, who died in 1956, put

these words into the mouth of one of his heroes:

'I am because someone dreams me; a man who sleeps and dreams and sees me acting, living and moving—and who is dreaming at this moment as I am speaking to you. When he dreams, I awake to life; when he awakes, my existence vanishes. I am a whim of his inspiration, a creation of his mind, a visitor in his nightly fantasies.'

10

Time Out

We have all experienced the misty grey monotony of a motorway in the early hours of the morning. Nothing seems real, time doesn't count. Not a sound reaches our ears except the insistent note of the engine. The white lane-lines unreel endlessly, hypnotically towards us. Are we really moving, or are we floating, fragments of dreams slipping past us? Fragments of memory – laughter out of the long-forgotten past. Faces mingle with the whispering leaves of a tree, a garden table splashed with sunshine, our parents, long-since dead, whom we hear talking to us as children. Specks of colour in the grey of the morning. The white thread unravels before us. Watch out! There's something on the road. Now it's gone. Just imagination – nothing but a waking dream.

As soon as external stimuli are greatly reduced or completely eliminated we lose our sense of time and reality.

Aviators who travel for hours at great altitudes above the clouds are particularly strongly affected by this feeling of being cut loose from reality. Dr A. H. Bennett of the R.A.F. Institute for Aviation Medicine has made a special study of the phenomenon. He took statements from a large number of pilots who indicated that at great altitudes they had the feeling that time no longer existed. They could no longer grasp the fact that they were sitting in an aeroplane. Everything had lost its meaning, all sense of place had vanished and they saw things remotely, as if through a long tunnel.

The American neurophysiologist and psychoanalyst John C. Lilly himself underwent a particularly rigorous test of the effects of the elimination of external stimuli – otherwise known as sensory deprivation. When he carried out the experiment in 1953 he was on the administrative staff of the American National Institute of Mental Health.

In order to achieve maximum sensory deprivation he had himself hung upside down, wearing a diving mask, in a container of water which was kept at blood temperature. He could see nothing, and apart from the lapping of the water and the faint noise of the breathing apparatus he could hear nothing either.

After the experiment was over, Lilly reported that he had felt practically weightless and had had a feeling of being carried away, like a corpse floating on water. In the first three-quarters of an hour Lilly's thoughts centred on everyday events and the experiment, but after about two hours these changed into daydreams and fantasies of an emotional character. According to Lilly they were too intimate to be discussed openly. After about two and a half hours of the experiment, a 'black curtain' was raised before his eyes, and a kind of three-dimensional film began to run before his mind's eye in speeded-up motion, in which strangely shaped small objects came and went, and a tunnel bathed in blue light appeared.

This vision of a tunnel is frequently seen in cases of sensory deprivation, whether by aviators flying high above the clouds, subjects in scientific experiments, or even people who are clinically dead but are subsequently brought back to life. The last category in particular often report having seen a tunnel, and these reports are often adduced as proof that there is life after death. In fact the experience proves very little, since total brain death does not occur until some hours after the heart has stopped.

A group of researchers at the University of Pittsburgh, Harry Braun, Robert Patten and Charles Vaughan, carried out an experiment to discover whether sensory deprivation in apes would produce the same fantasies in the waking state as it does in man.

The first step was the laborious task of training the apes to press a button or lever as soon as they saw fantasy images. The animals were made to sit on a stool in a glass cabin equipped with automats dispensing food and drink. Pictures were projected on a screen in front of them, and they had to react by pressing a lever, which operated the automats. If they failed to do so immediately, they received an electric shock on the leg. The slides used for the purpose showed food, dot patterns, humans and natural scenes. Slowly the apes learned to react regularly and promptly to pictorial impressions. Eventually their reaction time for pressing the levers was down to three thousandths of a second.

In the next phase of the experiment they were shut in the cabins for several days. They wore contact lenses which only transmitted a diffuse grey light, and the only noise they could hear was the monotonous murmur of a waterfall. The researchers now sat back and waited for the animals to have hallucinations, but found that instead the apes went quietly to sleep, one after the other. At first they moved their eyes rapidly to and fro, like a man scanning the lines of a newspaper; simultaneously they pressed their levers in rapid succession as if they were seeing images. This state lasted for some time and simultaneously they made faces, blew through their nostrils and breathed heavily. Since they pressed the levers and buttons in their sleep they were presumably under the influence of dreams. When the experiment was over, the researchers tested the animals' reactions again, in case the apparent evidence of their dreaming had been coincidental. However, this was clearly not the case, since as soon as they saw the pictures projected on the screen again, they operated their levers as they had been taught to.

Innumerable experiments have been carried out on the effects of sensory deprivation, and an equally large number on the extent to which electrical stimulation of the brain can influence behaviour. The manipulation of the human brain through suggestion or hypnosis and drugs reaches far back into history; by contrast the science of electrical stimulation of the brain is still in its infancy.

The first attempt to influence the operation of the brain electrically was made in 1898 by the Strasbourg physiologist Professor R. Ewald. He had devised a method of wiring the brain of a dog to a battery which he always carried with him.

However, the real bases of the electrical manipulation of animal and human behaviour were laid by the Swiss physiologist Walter Rudolf Hess. He carried out the first experiments of this kind on cats in 1924. Using a technique worthy of any modern horror film, he anaesthetized the cats and drilled a hole in their skull, then fed in fine electrical wires until they penetrated the brain matter. A weak electrical current was passed through the uninsulated wires, stimulating the surrounding area of the brain. The cats immediately became aggressive; their ears went back, their fur stood on end and their tails switched to and fro, and they slashed with their paws at a non-existent enemy. Hess called this electrically produced outburst of aggression 'mock rage'. By electrically stimulating the area of the brain concerned with eating, he also managed to produce 'mock hunger'. This artificially produced hunger made the cats eat everything they could get hold of, even inedible substances. Their appetites seemed inexhaustible, even directly after a meal.

Another decisive step forward in brain manipulation was

made by the American brain researcher José M. R. Delgado of Yale University. By devising a system of wireless transmission of electronic commands to electrodes implanted in the brain he inaugurated a new era which many people will view with mixed feelings. The Spanish-born researcher's forays into 'remote control' bullfighting contributed much to the dubious reputation which he acquired in the late 1950s and early 1960s.

Armed only with a transistorized push-button transmitter, Delgado faced a fighting bull in the arena of the Spanish town of Córdoba. The spectators held their breath as he flapped a red cape at it in true torero fashion. Nothing happened for some time, then the beast suddenly charged at Delgado with lowered horns, snorting with rage. It looked quite unstoppable, and Delgado seemed about to be gored at any moment, but suddenly the bull stopped dead in mid-charge – become as docile as an ox at the press of a button. What Delgado had done was to implant electrodes in the frontal lobe of the bull's brain, enabling him to control its actions with his transistorized transmitter – just like a model aircraft.

The thought that human behaviour could be controlled by electronic impulses in the same manner opens up frightening prospects. The range of feelings which can be artificially induced covers every possible shade of animal and human emotion; love or hate, naked anxiety or aggression, docility, cowardice, rage, panic, pleasure or extreme sexual behaviour – there is practically nothing which cannot be produced by manipulation.

Delgado carried out a large number of experiments which proved just how manipulable the brain is. One of his subjects was a five-year-old chimpanzee named Carlo. In a typical experiment Carlo could be seen to leap suddenly at a female sibling and chase her round their enclosure, growling angrily. After a good fifteen minutes of this the uproar subsided as suddenly as it had started. Carlo sat peacefully in his corner pulling faces.

Outside the cage, Delgado had been transmitting electrical impulses to electrodes in the chimpanzee's brain which controlled its behaviour. Both the senseless rage and the sudden docility had been artificially produced.

Delgado is not the only researcher to have manipulated the brains of experimental animals. Scientists are carrying out similar experiments in laboratories all over the world, in the hope of localizing brain functions and understanding them better. Their main object is a more precise diagnosis of disease, but Delgado has assured us that there is no difference between animals and men, and that every reaction which can be produced in apes by electrical stimulation of the brain could be reproduced in human beings.

According to the American neuropsychiatrist Perry London, no one can foresee the limits of development in this field, but what has already been achieved is already enough to cause considerable anxiety among the initiated and we should all be well aware of what is happening.

The Canadian James Olds had succeeded in producing feelings of pleasure in rats' brains by means of electrical impulses back in 1953, and Delgado built on these experiments. He taught rhesus monkeys to excite the pleasure centres of their brains electrically at the touch of a key so that they could induce feelings of pleasure in themselves whenever they wanted to. The monkeys' reactions were indescribable. They stimulated themselves continuously, often as many as three times a second, and went on operating the keys until they collapsed in total exhaustion. As soon as they had recovered a little they started again. They would endure anything, including pain and hunger, and lived only for the pleasure-inducing keys. Delgado described his subjects as playthings driven by a force beyond their control.

There are some emotions and visions which can be pro-

duced not only by electrical stimuli but also to a considerable degree by drugs. The American psychiatrist Roy Whit-
man and his colleagues at the University of Cincinnati tried to
discover the influence which certain drugs would have on
dreams. They started by observing a patient from the psy-
chiatric section under laboratory conditions for eight nights
in succession. Then they gave him the muscle relaxant and
tranquillizer meprobamate for another week and compared
the results. EEG and EOG recordings were made throughout
both the periods. When the recordings from the periods with
and without drugs were compared, there seemed at first
glance to be no fundamental difference. However, closer
investigation revealed that the patient slept more uneasily
during the nights when he was given meprobamate, although
the REM phases were not suppressed.

Drugs and intoxicants have a long history. Primitive
peoples have used them since time immemorial, and they
were originally treated not as an indulgence but as a
component of magical practices and ritualistic ceremonies.
Priests used intoxicants to put themselves into a state of
ecstasy.

While the Siberian shamans embarked on their journeys to
the land of dreams with the help of the poisonous fly-agaric
mushroom, the Aztecs and Mayas intoxicated themselves
with the 'meat of the gods' – the mushroom Teonanacatl and
the convolvulus Olodiuqui. The Indonesians intoxicate
themselves with kava, and the Mexicans drink pulque, which
is extracted from agaves. The Western and Central African
peoples chew cola nuts, while in Southern Asia, New Guinea,
Melanesia and on the East African coast, betel, from the
betel-nut palm, fulfils the same purpose. The favourite drink
of the Turkish and Mongolian peoples, on the other hand, is
the highly intoxicating fermented mare's milk.

Hashish and opium were both known in ancient times,
when they were used in medicine and for religious

ceremonies. In European history, too, preparations containing opium became increasingly important in medicine for combating illness and alleviating pain. In eighteenth-century England, for example, opium was given dissolved in alcohol. It was not known then that opium is addictive. Not until the nineteenth-century was it discovered that drugs can create both physical and psychological dependence, and of course in the twentieth-century drug addiction has become a universal phenomenon.

In the Romantic era many poets and writers saw drugs as a means of stimulating their imagination. S. T. Coleridge's poem 'Kubla Khan', for example, was written under the influence of opium, and Thomas De Quincey's *Confessions of an English Opium Eater* describe the writer's own experiences.

Many famous European intellectuals sought refuge in drugs from their pessimism, boredom and a sense of their own decadence. The sick, world-weary French poet Charles Baudelaire hoped to find the paradise which had eluded him in life itself in hashish and opium intoxication. Balzac, Maupassant, Lorrain, Heine, Poe and Oscar Wilde all used drugs, the effects of which were reflected in their works. The German poet Gottfried Benn in his early years believed that he must destroy the consciousness of self in order to penetrate to the primeval state of true being, and was prepared to use cocaine if all else failed. The dreamlike images of the Austrian expressionist poet Georg Trakl clearly reveal him as a drug addict, while Jean Cocteau related his own experiences as an addict in his work *Opium*. Aldous Huxley's book *The Doors of Perception* was the result of experiments with drugs, and the German writer Ernst Jünger is another of many who have described the effects of drugs, in his book *Drogen und Rausch*.

The general public first became fully aware of the dangers of drug-taking with the discovery of synthetic narcotics. The story begins on 16 April 1943, when Dr Albert Hofmann, a chemist at the Sandoz works in Basle, was working in his laboratory on a derivative of ergot, a fungus which attacks grain.

Sandoz had already successfully marketed ergot derivatives for the treatment of migraine and for use during pregnancy. On the day in question Hofmann had to go home in the early afternoon, because he felt dizzy and restless. When he got home he immediately lay down and sank into a state resembling drunkenness. Fantastic pictures passed before his closed eyes; they were remarkably three-dimensional, brilliant and multi-coloured. After some two hours the state passed – Hofmann had just experienced his first acid trip.

He remembered that he had been working with three chemicals, the effects of two of which he was familiar with. The third must have somehow got into his system. He had discovered it with the help of a colleague five years previously, but as experiments with animals had not produced any interesting results it had been set aside. In fact it was the twenty-fifth compound in the series of lysergic acids, which for this reason was called LSD-25 (lysergic acid diethylamide).

When Hofmann returned to work the following week he took what he considered to be a very small quantity of this new chemical and noted its effects: 'Slight feeling of dizziness... inability to concentrate... uncontrollable laughter...'

That evening Hofmann rode the 7 km to his home on a bicycle – there were no cars because of the war. He described his acid trip as follows: 'Everything in my field of vision swam to and fro, like the reflections in a distorting mirror at a funfair. The faces around me looked like grotesque, coloured masks.'

At the same time Hofmann was fully aware of his state. He observed himself as if he were an impartial bystander, hearing himself shouting like a madman and then abruptly

mumbling incomprehensible nonsense. Later he reported
that he intermittently felt detached from his body and that
sounds were transformed into visual experiences. Every
sound or noise produced a corresponding image, changing
kaleidoscopically in shape and colour.

Hofmann's experiment inaugurated the era of synthetic
'psychedelics'. Research went into high gear and in the next
twenty years over 1200 works on LSD were published. By the
1960s, however, the possession of LSD was forbidden by law
in many countries and its original manufacturers, Sandoz,
abandoned its production and distribution.

In the same period an LSD cult spread quickly, en-
couraged by figures such as the former Dean of Harvard,
Timothy Leary. For some years he was hailed as the prophet
of LSD, preaching a new religion based on the mind-expan-
ding properties of the drug. His slogan was 'Turn on, tune in,
drop out'. The cult soon died out in the early 1960s, as Leary
had become more interested in achieving an expansion of
consciousness through non-chemical means. Nevertheless,
the use of LSD and other drugs continues to increase steadily,
and has become an international problem.

LSD is violent in its effects. They start with waves of heat
and cold, accompanied by feelings of sickness, nausea and
dizziness. Visual images become distorted and distances
appear exaggerated, changing unpredictably. Patches of
light, coloured patterns and distorted hallucinatory images
appear. Dream-like experiences involving shifts in the con-
ventional time-scale are a characteristic feature of the LSD
experience. Now – the present moment – seems to stretch
into eternity, but is experienced at one remove. Occasionally
subjects feel a sense of mystical union with nature and the
universe, but these invariably disappear before the trip is
over. Often, however, the subject finds himself in a world of
horror, nightmares and psychosis – a truly apocalyptic experience.

Electrical stimulation and synthetic drugs are not the only means of affecting consciousness. A considerably older method is that of hypnosis. This technique was familiar to the shaman or witch-doctor, who would send his fellow tribesmen into a trance by monotonous chanting. The ancient world was familiar with the power of suggestion and used it in healing and religious ritual. But all this lay forgotten in the past when Mesmer revived the practice in the eighteenth century.

Franz Anton Mesmer, founder of the doctrine of animal magnetism – also known as Mesmerism – was born in 1734 in Iznang on Lake Constance. He was brought up in a seminary and studied theology, intending to become a Jesuit. He discovered that he was far more interested in science, however, and switched to medicine, obtaining a doctorate in Vienna in 1765 for his treatise *De Planetarium Influxu* ('On the Influence of Planets'). This thesis was based on the idea that a universal magnetic fluid – a secret magnetic force – binds together the heavenly bodies, the earth and all forms of life.

Mesmer believed that illnesses were the result of an imbalance in the bodily fluid, which could be corrected by the healing power of magnetism. His theory soon attracted the attention of Pater Maximilian Hehl, astronomer to the court of the Empress Maria Theresia. Believing that the human organism was influenced by the magnetism of the planets, Hehl had had some magnets made in the form of bodily organs which were intended to work against disturbing influences and combat illness. He had in fact succeeded in curing nervous illnesses by this method, and gave some of his magnets to Mesmer, who proceeded to use them on his own patients. A series of notable cures confirmed Mesmer in his theory, and gradually the public began to take notice of him.

Mesmer subsequently encountered the former monk Johann Gassner, who regarded illness as a form of demonic

possession, which he successfully 'drove out' by means of
exorcism. As he watched Gassner at work, it occurred to
Mesmer that magnets were superfluous for the successful
transmission of magnetic forces, and that the healing force
could be more effectively extracted from the healer's nervous
system through his hands. Mesmer concluded that his animal
magnetism, his healing power, could be communicated by
stroking and the laying on of hands, and then transmitted to
others through a suitable medium.

Hehl disagreed totally with Mesmer's new theory. Mesmer
fell into general disfavour and left Vienna for Paris, where he
soon established an extensive practice. His steadily expanding circle of patients threatened to overwhelm him, but
being of an inventive nature, he developed an apparatus
which enabled him to treat a number of patients at the same
time. He sat his patients around an apparatus consisting of a
wooden tub filled with water, tubes, iron filings and bottles of
·special magnetized water. The patients were connected to one
another by moist threads, and iron conducting bars led from
the tub to make contact with the diseased part of each patient's
body.

In this way Mesmer was able to magnetize up to thirty
patients at a time. His surgery was lined with mirrors and
carefully lit to create a mysterious atmosphere, which was
enhanced by sweet-smelling perfumes. Mesmer moved among
his patients like a magician, dressed in a purple robe and
accompanied by soothing music. Carrying an iron staff, he
and his helpers passed from one patient to another, stroking
them and performing strange hand movements over their
heads. Usually the treatment created a highly charged
emotional atmosphere which was transmitted from one
patient to another, culminating in violent convulsions.

Mesmer's method of treatment was apparently successful
and he was soon the talk of Paris. Louis XVI took notice of
him and created two committees to conduct a thorough

investigation into animal magnetism and its use. Among the members of the first committee was Dr Joseph-Ignace Guillotin, whose new invention, the guillotine, was to ensure a speedy and painless passage into the afterlife for so many members of the French aristocracy.

The first committee found that Mesmer's cures were real enough, but that the cause of them was extremely unclear. Mesmer's technique included the use of magnetized trees, which the patients had to touch, and the investigators objected that some of them had touched non-magnetized trees but had been cured nevertheless. Others had touched an ordinary lead disc, thinking that it was a magnetized nickel disc, and had been cured also. These experiments led the investigators to conclude that the so-called animal fluid could not be registered by the senses, and could have no effect either on the patients or on the members of the investigating board. At the same time, it was thought by no means impossible that this fluid could adversely affect public morale. The medical profession was forbidden to use Mesmer's methods under threat of suspension.

The second committee also unanimously rejected mesmerism, with one exception. The botanist Laurent de Jussieu refused to sign the official report and made a statement of his own to the effect that an invisible medium could be transmitted from one person to another and have a verifiable effect.

Despite this negative reception of animal magnetism and the official discrimination which followed, Mesmer became increasingly popular. He continued working in Paris until the outbreak of the French Revolution, when he closed his practice and after a short stay in Germany returned to Vienna. But here too his stay was soured by his being thrown in prison for two months on suspicion of spying. He left Austria and settled on Lake Constance, where he died in the year 1815.

In France, mesmerism had become established despite the Revolution, and a substantial number of mesmeric societies had been founded. Doctors had begun to recognize mesmerism in other countries, too. In Prussia, a doctor named Carl Wolfart declared his support for mesmerism, and was later made professor of mesmerism at the Berlin Academy. He also became the head of a new 'magnetic clinic', where he instructed many of Europe's leading doctors in Mesmer's method of healing.

One of Mesmer's French pupils, the Marquis de Puységur, even rediscovered the secret of the sleep rituals of the ancient world when he found that mesmerism could be used to send a patient into a sleep-like state.

The discovery came purely by chance. Puységur lived in seclusion on his estate of Busancy in the Champagne region and treated the local peasants for nothing. One day a young shepherd came to him, and while he was being treated fell repeatedly into a sleep-like state. The doctor was amazed to find that while in this state the youth was still able to answer questions which were put to him. When asked what was hurting him, the shepherd answered that his stomach was badly inflamed, and went on to describe the cure to be used in minute detail. Puységur had made notes of everything the patient said, and treated him according to the suggestion made while he was 'asleep'. The shepherd got well.

Fired by this experience, Puységur now proceeded to experiment with other patients, and enlisted the aid of the shepherd, since he wished to discover whether he would also be able to diagnose other people's illnesses while he was 'asleep'. He was amazed to find that this was in fact the case. In fact, Puységur discovered that subjects in a state of artificially induced somnambulism, or deep hypnosis, could be controlled and their actions guided by the hypnotist. On waking from their trance they often had no idea what had happened.

Writing in his memoirs in 1784, Puységur stated that the magnetic force would only be transmitted to the patient through the will of the healer, and that the patient would of necessity submit to mesmeric control.

In the same year the practice of mesmerism was prohibited by the medical society of the Académie des Sciences, but despite this the interest in animal magnetism in France and Germany grew steadily greater. Puységur's own interpretation of mesmerism eventually achieved general recognition, and after 1815 spread all over Europe. Baron du Potet, who had already made a name for himself by carrying out painless operations with the help of mesmerism, caused a further sensation when he announced that he and his colleague Dr Husson had succeeded in inducting somnambulism at a distance solely by the use of will-power.

Between 1826 and 1831 mesmerism in France was again subjected to official scrutiny. This time a committee of the Académie Royale de la Médecine had been given the task of investigating Husson's claims. Since Husson himself was both a member of the committee and the author of the committee's report, it seemed safe to assume that this time mesmerism would be recognized as a legitimate method of medical treatment, and receive the official seal of approval. This, however, was not the case. The Academy thought very differently from Husson and refused to print his official report of the committee's findings.

The intellectual climate in Germany was somewhat different, and here the idea of animal magnetism fell on more fertile ground. It was practised in England also, despite the opposition of the medical profession, and in the tolerant atmosphere of America it lasted until 1830. When the English surgeon John Elliotson met Baron du Potet in 1837 he immediately grasped the possibilities of mesmerism and began to use it as a means of anaesthesia and in the treatment of nervous disorders at University College Hospital, of which he was the founder. In 1843 he published the first number of *Zoist*, a journal devoted to the phenomenon of animal magnetism and its methods of application.

However, even Elliotson did not escape the opposition of his more conservative professional colleagues. In 1856, the board of University College Hospital passed a resolution banning all further use of mesmerism. Elliotson immediately resigned both his post as chief surgeon at the hospital and the chair of medicine at London University. He gave as the reason for his resignation that such an institution had been established for the discovery and dissemination of truth, and all other considerations should be subordinate to this.

Elliotson subsequently founded his own hospital in which mesmerism was used. In treating his patients, he now found that they could perceive sensations such as smells and pains which he himself experienced even when there was no personal contact between them. Elliotson demonstrated this before witnesses, but only succeeded in attracting more embittered attacks. Despite his energetic attempts at justifying himself, he was denounced as a madman and a charlatan, and towards the end of his life he tragically lost his hypnotic powers.

The case of another English surgeon, W. S. Ward, is equally indicative of the hidebound attitude of medical institutions at the time. Ward amputated the thigh of a patient under hypnosis, but when he reported the fact to the Royal Society of Medicine the whole thing was rejected as a fairy-tale and all the copies of Ward's report were destroyed. It was even suggested that the patient had been trained beforehand to withstand pain, and had only pretended not to feel anything when his leg was removed.

The celebrated English surgeon James Braid attended a demonstration given in London by the Swiss mesmerist Lafontaine with the intention of exposing him as a fraud, but found himself convinced by the phenomenon. Although he disagreed with contemporary theories on how it worked, Braid used mesmerism from 1842 onwards with great success. After long experience, he came to the conclusion that the trance state depended solely on the patient's suggestibility and not on the use of special magnetized objects. In expressing this opinion he attracted the opposition not only of his orthodox professional colleagues but also of other mesmerists committed to the traditional point of view. With the passage of time, however, his theory came to be accepted, and was finally adopted by the school of Nancy in France, which developed it further. Our present-day ideas about hypnotism have their origins in Braid's discovery.

Braid was the first person to coin the term neuro-hypnosis, which is now shortened to hypnosis. The technique was already being used successfully elsewhere, most notably by Dr James Esdaile in Calcutta. Esdaile read about hypnotism in Elliotson's journal, *Zoist*, and decided to try it in an operation on an Indian convict. The operation was successful and as a result the Governor of Bengal put Esdaile in charge of a hospital where he could continue his research. Between 1845 and 1851 he successfully used hypnosis as a means of anaesthesia in thousands of operations, including several hundred major surgical cases involving the removal of tumours and cataracts as well as amputations.

Esdaile too was continually attacked by the Indian medical press until his retirement. In England, *The Lancet* decried his successes, denouncing mesmerism as sheer humbug, not worthy of anyone's attention. Its adherents, the journal suggested, were nothing but frauds and charlatans, who should be driven out of the medical profession. Any practising doctor who sent a sick patient to a mesmerist quack deserved to have no more patients for the rest of his days.

When chloroform was discovered in 1848, interest in hypnosis in England and the United States rapidly faded. In Europe, however, research continued. In 1882 the French doctor Liébeault used hypnosis to cure a chronic case of sciatica which had previously been treated by the famous neurologist H. Bernheim of the medical faculty at Nancy. Bernheim was so impressed by the cure that he studied hypnosis, despite his initial reservations, and founded a school for the study and application of the technique.

The followers of Liébeault and Bernheim both belong to what is known as the Nancy school, while the so-called Paris school goes back to the famous neurologist Jean Martin Charcot of the Salpêtrière hospital. The basic difference between these two schools rests on two main points. The Nancy school maintained that hypnosis is based on suggestion, while the Paris school considered the cause to be physical. Also, Charcot maintained that hypnosis could only be used successfully in neurotic patients, with the corollary that it must always be connected with morbid hysteria.

The two opposing parties decided their dispute by means of a public demonstration. Bernheim and Liébeault proved clearly and unequivocally that normal subjects are easier to hypnotize than unstable ones and that hypnosis does not require mechanical aids such as the magnets used by Mesmer. Despite this blow to Charcot's theories, his studies on hypnosis retained a certain influence. Sigmund Freud, who was Charcot's pupil at La Salpêtrière for some time, acknowledged his teacher's contribution to a better understanding of hysteria.

Many people still consider hypnosis a fraud. Even in scientific circles every attempt has been made to play down this area of knowledge and bring it into disrepute, and people's ideas on the subject are still unclear today, although it has more than proved its worth as a therapeutic technique. Its main advantage is that it provides a relatively swift and sure means of access to the subconscious. Basically, hypnosis is a form of sleep – a dream-like state in which a skilled hypnotist can guide the course of events.

There is a basic distinction to be made between light and deep hypnosis. Practically everyone can be hypnotized if the right technique is used. In deep hypnosis practically any suggestion will be carried out by the subject so long as it does not conflict with his conscience. In other words, the commands received under hypnosis must be morally acceptable.

At the 3rd International Congress on Psychology and Psychiatry in Munich, a Lausanne specialist by the name of Dr Bonjour reported that he had induced a premature delivery by means of hypnosis. As his patient was in considerable pain, Bonjour decided that it was essential to induce the birth weeks before it was due. He therefore put the pregnant woman under hypnosis and made the suggestion that she would bring her child into the world in three days' time.

After three days, the woman did indeed have the child, but when she was woken from her hypnosis, she had no idea that she had already given birth.

A person who responds easily to suggestion can suddenly fall into an REM state when he is ordered to dream under hypnosis.

Experiments of this kind were carried out at the Medical School of the University of Pennsylvania by B. Brady and B. S. Rosner. Subjects who responded to the order to dream under hypnosis were observed to make eye movements characteristic of REM sleep. When the unhypnotized subjects being used as a control were told to dream, they also had dream-like fantasies, but the REM phases were nothing like as strong as in the hypnotized subjects.

We seldom remember our REM dreams, because they slip from our memory within a minute of their ending. The experience of hypnotized dreamers is very different. In the experiments carried out by Brady and Rosner they could still clearly remember the details of a dream when they were woken from hypnosis ten minutes after the end of the REM phase. From this it may be concluded that people who respond easily to hypnosis are more able to 'put on' REM phases and direct their states of consciousness than others.

The American psychologist Johann Stoyva, of the medical faculty at the University of Colorado, also carried out a number of instructive experiments. He made post-hypnotic suggestions to his subjects before they went to sleep that they should dream of particular events. A post-hypnotic suggestion is one which is made to the subconscious during hypnosis and later carried out after the subject has come out of hypnosis, in this case during sleep. Stoyva used the EEG method in his experiments and found that in 70–100 per cent of cases, the dreams suggested by the experimenter coincided with the accounts subsequently given by the subjects. There were inevitably small deviations and embellishments in the actual dreams, but basically the content which had been suggested was clearly recognizable. The REM phases in which these dreams took place did not last as long as in normal dreaming occurring without hypnosis. When dreams were suggested to particularly responsive hypnotic subjects and the latter were woken from non-REM phases, it was found that their accounts of their dreams coincided fully with the experimenters' hypnotic suggestions. In experiments carried out by another scientist it proved impossible to suppress REM sleep completely by means of hypnosis.

Practically anything can be experienced through suggestion. Under hypnosis we can even become time-travellers, returning to the past and experiencing it anew in the minutest detail. In hypnosis as in dreaming, any other 'reality' can become as convincing and acceptable as the present one – so long as it has been suggested. We are all constantly hypnotized to a greater or lesser degree by the sights and sounds of everyday life – traffic lights, television commercials, music, political speeches or our superior's orders at work.

Under deep hypnosis – usually produced by the constant

repetition of a single insistent suggestion, which effects a change in the alpha rhythm in the brain – we can feel as light as a feather, or as heavy as a block of concrete. We can be totally oblivious of pain or lose our memory. As in dreaming, we can be taken out of our own time and fall into some other 'time trap' that has been suggested to us and then return from that place of no-time to the present.

Do such places really exist? Are such 'time-slips' really possible? One might think so from the case of a Spanish soldier in Manila. On 24 October 1953 he was on sentry duty in the Philippine capital, and twenty-four hours later he found himself in Mexico City, over 9000 miles away, without having the least idea how he had got there, or why.

Something similar happened to nineteen-year-old Bruce Burkan. On 24 October 1967 he was found sitting at a bus terminus in Newark, U.S.A., dressed in a badly cut suit with only seven cents in his pocket. He had no idea why he was sitting there or what had happened to him in the past two months.

On 22 August Burkan had driven to Asbury Park beach in New Jersey with his girl-friend. He was wearing nothing but a pair of swimming trunks. At the beach Burkan had left his girl-friend to go and fetch something. When he didn't come back she became anxious and went to look for him. Unable to find him, she went to the parking lot to see if he was there, but the car was locked and still in the same place where they had left it. There was no trace of Burkan anywhere. His parents immediately initiated a public search for him but none of their appeals produced any result. Eventually they were convinced that their son had met with some accident and they finally decided to hold a memorial service for him.

When Burkan reappeared two months later he was unable to remember what had happened in the intervening period. According to reporters, however, he repeatedly emphasized how disturbed he was that no one had recognized or seen him after the public appeals despite the fact that his bright red hair made him immediately noticeable. He felt as though the time between 22 August and 24 October had ceased to exist.

Something equally inexplicable happened to Chester Archey, an American policeman with fifteen years in the service. On a warm August night in 1966 he was patrolling his usual beat in the northern quarter of Philadelphia, in the state of Pennsylvania, when he suddenly found himself in a completely strange town called Pennsauken in New Jersey. He drove around in bewilderment and became involved in an accident. In his deposition at the subsequent police hearing, Archey said that he had not the slightest idea how he had got to Pennsauken and didn't even know where it was.

Not only individual people but whole groups of them have vanished suddenly. One of the first colonies in the United States suffered this fate. This was founded in the year 1585 on the island of Roanoke off the coast of present-day North Carolina. The whole colony disappeared, never to be seen again, and with it the first child to be born on the American continent of European parents – a girl named Virginia Dare.

During the First World War a whole British regiment was lost in a few minutes near Suvla Bay in Turkey. A detachment of English soldiers watching from a trench stated under oath that they had seen the 14th Norfolk Regiment march into a strange brownish cloud which lay right across their path. None of them reappeared on the other side. After a while the cloud rose slowly from the ground and joined other similar clouds, which all moved off against the wind. Not one of the 800 soldiers in the regiment was ever seen again. They had simply disappeared from the face of the earth.

In northern Canada the disappearance of a whole Eskimo settlement caused a sensation in August 1930. The Royal Canadian Mounted Police found the village completely deserted when they passed on a tour of inspection. Closer investigation revealed that although all thirty inhabitants had disappeared, all their supplies, clothing, kayaks, guns and dogs were still there. The Mounties were considerably surprised by this, for no Eskimo goes far from his settlement without taking his gun and his dog – his two most valuable possessions. The whole area was searched systematically in an operation lasting fourteen days, but not a single clue to their whereabouts was found. Strangest of all was the fact that a grave at the edge of the settlement had been opened and the body removed. The desecration of a grave is regarded as a particularly serious crime among Eskimos and it hardly seemed possible that the village's inhabitants had left their homes taking the dead man with them but leaving provisions, clothing, weapons and dogs.

Something very different happened to eleven-year-old Graciela del Lourdes Gimenez. On 4 August 1968 she was playing in the garden of her parents' house in Córdoba in Argentina. As she later told reporters, she was about to turn and go into the house when a cloud of white mist appeared in her path. This came nearer and nearer until she was unable to see the neighbouring houses, and unable even to turn and call out to her mother. She said that she had no idea what happened next, but that all of a sudden she was in a large square full of people. She went straight to the nearest house and knocked on the door, and the inhabitants took Graciela to the police. It was never explained how the child had managed to get from a suburb of Córdoba to the Plaza Espãna in the town centre.

On 23 September 1880 an American farmer named David Lang disappeared in the classic fashion – before the eyes of his family and friends. Lang owned a farm outside the town of Gallatin in Texas and was going from his house to the meadow to attend to the horses. From a distance, his wife and children, and some friends who had just arrived, saw him take a few steps across the meadow and suddenly disappear. The police were immediately called and started a search in which many of the townspeople spontaneously took part. Every square yard of the pasture was systematically searched and holes were even bored to see if there were any underground caves or mine shafts into which Lang could have fallen. But all their efforts were in vain, and Lang never reappeared.

Another farmer, Isaac Martin, disappeared on 3 April 1885 in a similarly inexplicable fashion. He too was going into one of his fields when he disappeared from the face of the earth.

An almost incredible story is that of seven-year-old Denis Martin, who in the summer of 1969 was visiting the Great Smoky Mountains with his father and some relatives. He was running along beside his father when he suddenly disappeared from one moment to the next. A mammoth search was undertaken: 1400 men combed the park, turning over every stone, searching every cleft in the rocks. But once again, all was in vain. The child was never found.

Another unexplained disappearance is that of two RAF officers in the Arabian desert. Pilot officer D. R. Stewart and Lieutenant W. T. Day had taken off on 24 July 1924 on a routine reconnaissance flight. When the machine failed to return a search party was sent out the following day and found the missing machine totally undamaged standing ready for take-off in the middle of the desert. There was plenty of fuel in the tanks, and there were no signs of a struggle or any other mishap. Two sets of footprints which ended abruptly a few steps away from the machine were the only traces ever found of the English airmen.

An aviation mystery which remained equally unexplained took place on 5 December 1945. This was the day on which five TBM Avenger torpedo bombers disappeared on a flight from the American Navy's base at Fort Lauderdale. They had taken off on a routine training mission with fourteen crew members when contact with the ground station was suddenly broken off. A US Navy flying boat with a thirteen-man crew was immediately dispatched to search for the missing Flight 19, but after twenty minutes in the air this machine too broke contact with the ground. In one afternoon six aircraft carrying a total of twenty-seven crew members had simply disappeared into thin air.

An extensive air, sea and land rescue operation was put into motion and dragged on for weeks with no result. The missing machines never turned up, and not a single scrap of wreckage, not even an oil slick on the water was found to mark their former existence.

It would be too simple to explain away all occurrences of this kind as the result of natural causes. They appear to involve an alteration in the space/time continuum, a phenomenon which does not fit in with our concept of reality. Everything seems to suggest that some of these vanished people were snatched from our present level of reality, just like the Minuteman missile.

It remains to be asked where they went to.

11

Unknown Dimensions

A team of American psychologists at Stanford University trained litters of kittens to see the world in stripes from birth. While some of them grew up in a horizontally striped world, the others lived in vertically striped surroundings. Later, when the cats became adults, they were able to roam around the laboratory in a perfectly normal fashion, yet they clearly believed that the world was actually divided into stripes – either horizontal or vertical – since these were the only impressions which had been received by their brains. The result was that the cats who saw horizontal stripes were living in an entirely different world from that inhabited by the cats who saw vertical stripes – each inaccessible to the other. For both categories, their own world was real, but for an observer from our 'normal world' both of their worlds were false.

This raises the question of how real our own world, the universe which we perceive, is, and whether other equally real worlds do not exist beyond the range of our perceptions.

We know that our universe consists of space, energy, matter and that all-pervasive yet elusive phenomenon time, and came into being about 5000 to 10,000 million years ago.

In 1927 the Belgian Abbé Lemaître came to the conclusion that our universe must have originated from one compressed original atom. All the innumerable galaxies were packed together in a state of unimaginable density in the form of subatomic particles. The density of this original atom must have been many times that of water, while the temperature must have been many thousands of millions of degrees. Most probably this cosmic egg consisted of neutrons compressed 'as far as they could go'. Then, at the beginning of time this cosmic egg was scattered in all directions by a gigantic primeval explosion. The causes of this cosmic explosion have yet to be fully explained. For the Abbé Lemaître there was doubtless no problem – the good God simply pressed the red button and set off the cosmic bomb.

Fragments from this 'big bang', as it was designated by the astrophysicist G. Gamow in a book which he published in 1948, condensed all over the universe into star systems of different sizes. Our own Milky Way with about 150,000 million stars, planets, moons and life forms – such as ourselves – originated in the debris of the big bang.

In general the galaxies are moving away from one another – a phenomenon first observed by the American astronomer E. P. Hubble – and the further away they are the greater is their velocity. From this general movement of the galaxies, originating in the big bang, scientists have derived the concept of an expanding universe. If the universe continues to expand into eternity, then the eventual result would be total emptiness.

This possibility is disputed by the American astrophysicist Professor Allan Sandage of the Mount Wilson Observatory. He believes that the expansion of our universe will continue for only another 83,000 million years before it once again comes to a standstill. According to Sandage this will be followed by a process of contraction. During the following 45,000 million years the universe will be drawn together again by the mutual attraction of the galaxies until a state of maximum density is reached – another primeval atom, which will be followed by another big bang in an endlessly recurring cyclic process.

The Maya of pre-Columbian America were obsessed by time and firmly believed in the principle of cyclic repetition. Their world, their whole concept of reality was arranged according to a complex calendar by which they regulated their lives. For the Maya, time was a magic circle, a round of never-ending duties to be performed. They constructed buildings and made decisions not according to necessity but because they were prescribed by the calendar. Every altar, every monument served to close the wheel of time, to stand as a reminder of time passing. But the most important principle in the life of the Maya was their belief in the cyclic nature of history. For them, yesterday, today and tomorrow were repeated throughout all eternity in a 260-year cycle.

For the Babylonians, time was inextricably bound up with the motion of the stars, which influenced the life and the fate of mankind. Among the Greeks, the Stoics believed that time was bound up with the fate of the cosmos, that the universe would eventually be extinguished, but would be recreated with everything which had ever existed. It was not until the coming of Christianity that the concept of linear time first appeared. In the Christian view of the world, the concept of cyclic repetitions is replaced by that of the Day of Judgement – time runs in a single line from the beginning of creation to the end of the world.

Opinions have long been divided on the nature of time and were especially so during the Middle Ages. Some believed in cyclic repetition, while others defended the concept of time as an ever-rolling stream. In a work written in 1638 the celebrated Italian mathematician and astronomer Galileo Galilei (1564–1642) turned against the concept of the wheel of time and pleaded in favour of a linear motion – time unfolding in a geometrically straight line. In his *Philosophiae Naturalis Principia Mathematica,* Isaac Newton (1642–1727) presupposed the existence of an absolute space, an absolute time and an absolute movement. These suppositions assumed a well-nigh canonical importance among physicists and• philosophers. Newton asserted that absolute time, because of its nature, always remained the same, independently and without reference to matter.

The work of the celebrated French mathematician J. Henri Poincaré (1854–1912) marked a turning point in scientific attitudes towards time. In 1904, at the Congress for Arts and Sciences in St Louis, Poincaré first mentioned the principle of relativity, though he was unable to put forward a complete theory. The first comprehensive theory of relativity was proposed a year later by Albert Einstein (1879–1955). In coming to grips with the concept of time, Einstein had first of all tried to reconcile the theory of electromagnetic light waves of the English physicist James Clerk Maxwell (1831–1879) with the rest of physics, which was based on the classical mechanics of Newton.

At that time it was still generally believed that an invisible substance known as ether was present in the universe through which light waves were transmitted, just like sound waves, which need a medium such as water, air or some solid material for their propagation.

In 1887 the American physicist Albert A. Michelson (who in 1907 became the first US scientist to receive the Nobel Prize) and E. Morley decided to try to prove the existence of the ether by measuring its movement in relation to the earth. This they thought could be done by simultaneously measuring the speed of light travelling in two different directions, and Michelson had developed an instrument which he called the interferometer for the purpose. To their amazement, the two physicists discovered that the speed of light remained the same no matter how the interferometer was oriented, a fact which seemed to conflict directly with the Newtonian law. Other experiments also proved that the speed of light is a universal constant.

Albert Einstein, who had taken an interest in this research because he too was concerned with the ether problem, then published his revolutionary theory of relativity in 1905. And with its appearance, our picture of the world, our concept of space and time was drastically changed over night. Before Einstein a metre had been a metre, the shortest distance between two points a straight line, and time an absolutely reliable and immutable process. It is thanks to Einstein that light became linked with time and time with space – and likewise energy with matter, matter with space and space with gravitation.

In order to illustrate the theory of relativity, let us imagine that a train is travelling across the countryside at 70 mph. On board is a fly, which is moving from the last coach towards the locomotive. In one of the compartments a passenger notes that the fly is flying forwards at a speed of 3 mph. As the train speeds through a small station a lynx-eyed traveller is watching from the platform. He sees the train passing at 70 mph and inside it the fly advancing at its own speed of 3 mph. The total speed of the fly relative to the traveller will thus be 73 mph. The passenger in the compartment, on the other hand, will see the station pass by at 70 mph.

At the next big station the train stops. Another train is standing on the opposite track with a passenger looking out of the window. One of the trains imperceptibly starts moving, but which one? Both passengers believe that it is the other train which is leaving the station.

The first passenger has been moving again for some time when an Inter-city express passes on the next track, travelling 30 mph faster than the other train. Our passenger's only point of reference is the carriages of the express moving past him, so he has no idea whether his own train has stopped and the express is passing at 30 mph, or whether the express has stopped, while his own train is moving backwards. The impression would be the same as that given by the true situation, which is that the first train is still travelling towards its destination at 70 mph, while the Inter-city is doing the same at 100 mph. Without some stationary point of reference, the traveller is completely unable to describe the situation correctly.

Thus we can never talk of absolute movement, only of movement relative to something else. Even an observer cannot take it for granted that he is stationary. Thus Einstein's theory of relativity is based on the principle that all movement is relative.

Everything in the universe is in motion. The earth is revolving both on its own axis and around the sun. The latter is also moving in relation to other stars in the Milky Way, while the Milky Way too is moving, in relation to other galaxies. There is no single star which can serve as a stationary point of reference.

From the relativity of movement and his fundamental conclusion that the speed of light always remains constant in relation to the observer, at about 300,000 km per second, Einstein deduced that the existence of the ether cannot be proved. The Irishman G. F. Fitzgerald and the Dutchman H. A. Lorentz had already put forward a concept which explained why this was so in 1892. According to their theory, known as the Fitzgerald-Lorentz contraction, an object contracts in the direction of its movement through space, i.e. through the ether. Translated into terms of our example this means that the passing train is shortened for the observer on the platform. If the train were travelling at half the speed of light – i.e. 150,000 km per second – and it was 100 metres long, the observer on the platform would see it as only 50 metres long.

But the most startling consequence of the theory of relativity is that time also can be influenced by movement. Time passes at a different rate for two observers who are moving in relation to one another. The situation opens up interesting possibilities. Let us suppose for example that some time in the future we succeeded in building an interstellar spaceship capable of travelling at 99 per cent of the speed of light. The hours on board such a spaceship would pass seven times more slowly than on earth, though the astronauts on board would not notice any difference. Moreover the astronauts would age seven time more slowly than their relatives who had stayed on earth. In recent years this property of time has in fact been proved by experiment.

The collision of protons from space and air molecules in the upper atmosphere of the earth produces so-called mu-mesons – very light elementary particles. Because of the colossal speed at which they approach the earth time for them passes seven times more slowly than it does for an observer on earth. Subjectively speaking their life-span is seven times longer than it is for the earthly observer.

There is another interesting experiment which effectively demonstrates the distortion of time. Two American physicists, J. Hafele and R. Keting flew twice round the earth in opposite directions, first to the east and then to the west.

They used four highly accurate atomic clocks, capable of registering the minutest differences in the passage of time, and their round-the-world trips entailed thirteen landings and take-offs, achieving a considerable degree of acceleration in relation to the earth. It turned out that the clocks which they took with them in the air ran at different speeds to those which they left on the ground. On the eastward trip they lost 50 nanoseconds (1 nanosecond = 1 thousandth of a millionth of a second), while on the westward trip they gained an equal amount.

As I have already suggested, the unreliability of our traditional notions of time will become particularly clear if one day astronauts are able to travel to other solar systems at near to the speed of light. Inside a spaceship, time passes more slowly. Paradoxically the space travellers do not notice anything themselves, but in relation to the people they left behind on earth they will have been subject to time dilation and when they return they will have taken a step into the future.

The nearer the speed of a spaceship to the speed of light, the greater will be the difference between the passage of time on earth and in the ship. If the latter is travelling through space at 96 per cent of light speed, the earth hour is reduced to 17 minutes. At 97 per cent of light speed it is only 15 minutes and at 98 per cent only 12 minutes. As soon as 99 per cent of light speed is reached only 6 of the earthly 60 minutes remain.

It has been said of both Newton and Einstein that it was their simple, almost childish approach to fundamental questions which led them to their revolutionary discoveries. Indeed, Einstein was one day told by his university teachers that he was a hopeless case. His general indifference and total lack of aptitude for anything at all were merely demoralizing the staff and his fellow students. Einstein left the university and from 1902 to 1907 worked in the Swiss patent office in Bern.

People would often ask how the most important scientific theory of our century could have been developed under circumstances such as these. Einstein's reply was that he had been preoccupied with the problem of the measurement of time since he was sixteen and his revolutionary ideas were the result of nearly ten years of mental effort and speculation. He had written down the results of his work without once referring to existing scientific research. Later, Einstein once said that theoretical physics can best be carried out by a plumber who is not constantly obliged to justify his existence by producing scientific discoveries and is therefore able to concentrate on the essential problems.

A vital link in the development of Einstein's ideas about time was provided by the Russian-German mathematician Hermann Minkowski (1864–1909) with his concept of space-time, which he first put forward in a now famous lecture at the 80th Congress of Natural Sciences at Cologne in 1908. Following in Einstein's footsteps, he pointed out that no one has ever perceived a particular place except at a particular time, nor a particular time except at a particular place. Minkowski combined the dimensions of space with the dimension of time to form a four-dimensional geometry of space-time which he called the space-time continuum.

On the basis of this model Einstein came to the conclusion that the structure of the objective, physical world is four-dimensional in nature, but its three spatial dimensions and one temporal dimension do not have the same significance for every observer.

In 1905 Einstein wrote in his theory of relativity that there can be no speed faster than the speed of light. An infinite amount of energy would be required to accelerate a particle to the speed of light and as there is no greater amount of energy conceivable than an infinite amount, the speed of light must be the absolute limiting factor in the universe.

Einstein notwithstanding, there have been heated arguments among scientists in recent years over the possible existence of so-called tachyons – particles travelling faster than the speed of light. The debate was started by the American physicists Olexa Myron Bilanuik, V.K. Deshpande and E.C. George Sudarshan of Rochester University, and by Gerald Feinberg, Professor of Physics at Columbia University.

It was long considered blasphemy to doubt that the speed of light was the absolute limiting velocity, and when tachyons were first mentioned there was a lengthy argument about whether their existence could be justified in terms of the theory of relativity. Eventually, however, they were admitted within the framework of the theory of relativity, since if tachyons exist they are formed at more than light speed and never fall below that velocity. Nevertheless they remain a problem, since they turn our whole picture of the world upside down, and for a particular reason. As soon as the speed of light is exceeded time starts to run backwards, and once this happens our whole concept of cause and effect has to be revised, since the effect will precede the cause.

Let us imagine the existence of a tachyon telephone – a device which may one day really exist. This tachyon telephone would be the best possible horoscope, for since tachyons are moving into the past they could bring us news from the future. We could ring ourselves up in order to find out what has happened in the future and thus avoid making incorrect decisions. A tachyon telephone would also be the ideal medium of communication with beings in other solar systems, if such should exist, for we would be able to communicate with them without a time lapse.

There is another extraordinary subatomic particle called a neutrino, which has neither mass nor electrical charge and which next to nothing can stop. Even if a lead shield could be devised as big as the whole solar system, a neutrino would pass through it as if it were butter. In fact we ourselves could be penetrated by a neutrino world inhabited by neutrino beings without being aware of the fact. It is just another facet of reality.

A neutrino world would be strange enough in itself. But the most mysterious place in the universe, and the most difficult to imagine, would undoubtedly be a so-called black hole. Black holes are the subject of a great deal of speculation, and are thought to have been formed roughly as follows.

We now know more or less for certain that a star is condensed from a cloud of gas. Its core heats up and it contracts under the force of gravity. At a certain critical temperature the hydrogen changes into helium in what is known as a hydrogen fusion reaction.

A star begins to shrink into a 'white dwarf' as soon as its nuclear fuel – the hydrogen – has been used up. In the case of our own sun, this will happen in approximately 6000 million years.

If the mass of a star exceeds 1.4 times that of our own sun – the limit set by the Indian astronomer Subrahmanyan Chandrasekhar – a supernova explosion occurs. As much as 10 per cent of the star is hurled into space while its core collapses with such sudden violence that the elementary particles in the star's atoms fuse into neutrons. The star shrinks to a diameter of only a few kilometres and consists mostly of neutrons packed tightly together. A few cubic centimetres of such a 'neutron star' would have a mass of several million tonnes.

However, if the shrunken, super-dense core of a large star has twice the mass of the sun then it cannot exist either as a white dwarf or as a pulsar. It continues to collapse inexorably, and it is now assumed by scientists that its mass finally overcomes the energy in the core, producing a total and catastrophic concentration of matter. The star becomes a 'black hole', a kind of gravity sink which sucks into it everything in the surrounding space. The question is, how does a black hole end? Where does the matter which is sucked in go to? Perhaps it is totally annihilated, or perhaps, as some scientists now assume, it leaves our universe altogether and reappears in another. But it seems just as likely that it should reappear in some other part of our own universe at another time from our own.

In a black hole time is stretched by gravity practically into eternity. John G. Taylor, Professor of Mathematics at London University, writes: 'The ergosphere of a large, rotating black hole, is the place to spend a while if one wants to travel thousands (or millions) of years into the future.'

According to one theory, matter which is swallowed up by a black hole reappears somewhere else as antimatter.

In 1963 great excitement was caused by the discovery of quasars – quasi-stellar radio sources which radiate enormously strong radio waves. Quasars are practically invisible, almost point-like objects whose unusual production of energy is still a mystery. Some scientists believe that quasars and radio galaxies are produced by the collision of matter and antimatter, but so far no one has been able to make a distinction between galaxies and anti-galaxies.

The English physicist Paul Dirac suggested back in 1928 that for every elementary particle there was an anti-particle – a kind of mirror image of matter. The first anti-particle was in fact discovered shortly after Dirac made his prediction, and christened the positron. It corresponds more or less to an electron, but unlike the latter carries a positive charge and spins in the opposite direction. Since Dirac first raised the subject, the question of what purpose antimatter could fulfil in the universe has been the subject of endless speculation.

Meanwhile in Russia, the development of nuclear physics led to the discovery of a new form of antimatter. Aluminium foil was bombarded with a proton beam – i.e, a beam of hydrogen atom nuclei – boosted to an energy of 70 million electron-volts by the proton accelerator at Serpukhov, south of Moscow. When these particles collided with the nuclei of the aluminium atoms, other nuclei were produced consisting of two antineutrons and one antiproton. These were anti-tritium nuclei – the mirror image of the nuclei of the radioactive hydrogen isotope tritium. Three years after this discovery the Russians succeeded in producing anti-helium nuclei at Serpukhov.

Since it has been proved that antimatter exists, scientists have had to consider the possibility that not only anti-stars and anti-galaxies but also an anti-universe exist also. The Russian physicist A. Sakharov supports the hypothesis that our present universe was created from an anti-universe which perished in a cosmic catastrophe some 30,000 million years ago. According to Sakharov this universe consisted primarily of antimatter which exploded after being compressed at very high temperatures. In the process of atomic disintegration which then followed more matter was created than anti-matter. And it was from these particles of matter, in Sakharov's opinion, that our universe was created.

Other scientists believe that an anti-universe with anti-stars exists side by side with our own. But however fascinating the idea of an anti-earth with anti-men on it may seem, we should perhaps remember that if man and anti-man should ever meet in a fraternal embrace, their substance would immediately be dissipated into energy with a loud explosion.

And how very strange a world of tachyon antimatter would be. Its inhabitants would live differently from us: they would live backwards, from the future into the past. They would be born old and grow younger from anti-day to anti-day. In their anti-world, cause would follow effect. The paradox is that anti-men would be convinced that they were growing older while we were growing younger and younger.

Somewhere perhaps an anti-man is lying in his anti-bed and dreaming an anti-dream. . .

'Once, towards morning, I had a cosmic dream,' relates the German dramatist Gerhart Hauptmann (1862–1946). 'I was confronted with perspectives of the most colossal differences of scale. I saw nothing less than the globe spinning in space. But I myself clung to it hopelessly like a dwindling, death-bound, minimal creature, every moment in danger of being flung off into infinite space.'

12

The Key

A soft alarm clock lies in the burning sand, melting and useless. Above it, naked in the endless wilderness, hangs a solitary, mysterious key.

Dali's painting suggests a variety of themes connected with our subject. The melting alarm clock is a timeless, unnatural image, in which time itself becomes a useless object. And the key is the archetypal image of life's mysteries, the revealer of secrets, the unlocker of doors into the unknown.

Raymond de Becker said:

> The great privilege of dreams is to bombard us with images until we have fully understood the inadequacy of our waking life and decide to employ them in realizing the wholeness which we are promised ... of one thing I am sure: that a systematic use of dreams, including new ways of inducing them, for cultural or artistic, therapeutic or analytical, motor or prospective ends would entail a profound modification of our vision of the world, an acceleration and enriching progress of history ... by placing the individual in the totality of the universal realities which condition him, it would wrest him from the absur-

dity of his existence and undoubtedly enable him to rediscover the meaning of life. One of the great duties of contemporary man is to learn how to dream again.

The sleep researcher Ann Faraday had a highly unusual dream one morning, in which she awoke from the same dream, got up and walked to and fro in her room. Everything seemed quite normal, with one exception – a window had suddenly appeared mysteriously in an internal wall. This one false note made her aware that she was not awake but dreaming. At the same time the thought came to her that she always advised her patients under similar circumstances simply to let dreams of this type run their course, without trying to influence them. Following her own advice, she looked out of this dream window, all the time aware that it wasn't really there and feeling slightly ridiculous as a result.

Her daughter's room was next door and so this was naturally what she expected to see through the window. But instead she saw herself sunk in contemplation of a stretch of grass covered with daisies, which seemed to merge into a forest of bluebells stretching as far as the eye could see. For a moment Ann Faraday was unable to get her bearings and thought that she was at the window of some English stately home, set among lawns which had been partly allowed to run wild. Finally she tore herself away from the spectacle and turned round. There was her bedroom, looking just the same as ever. For a moment Ann Faraday thought she must be sleepwalking, then she decided to make the best of her 'clairvoyance' and pummelled her bed with her fists to see if it was as solid as in her waking state. It felt just the same as it normally did. Then she saw her husband lying asleep in bed at her side. Because she wanted to know whether a human body can be touched and felt in a dream, she shook him awake and noticed that he was as normal and supple as usual. Now beginning to wonder whether she wasn't in fact awake, and had really woken up her husband, she suddenly saw herself lying curled up in bed, alone. Then she remembered that her husband had already got up hours beforehand.

Ann Faraday goes on to describe how she was suddenly flooded with strange bursts of energy and felt as though she were high. She had the feeling that her body was being carried away by this energy, on some interior journey. At the same time she was aware that she was asleep, for she could hear a dog barking in the neighbourhood, some workmen making a noise in the cellar, and the distant roar of traffic.

The American psychologist Charles Tart calls dreams involving deliberate perceptions of this type 'high dreams'. A high dream can be defined as one in which the sleeper perceives that he is in another world – the world of dreams. While dreaming he registers the fact that his state of consciousness has changed.

While in this state, Ann Faraday felt sympathy for the rest of humanity which could not share her unique experience. Finally she looked at her watch and saw with relief that she could continue dreaming for another fifteen minutes before her husband would wake her with a cup of coffee.

At that moment her husband actually entered the room with the coffee. Ann Farady now woke from her dream in reality and knew that everything she had so far experienced had merely been part of her dream – even her glance at her watch as she estimated the time she still had left.

Naturally she immediately related her dream experience to her husband, who immediately left the room and returned with a piece of paper on which he had noted a dream which he had had the same night. Some three hours earlier he had dreamed that his wife had shaken him awake because he was sleeping on the wrong side of the bed; he too had discovered a window in the wrong wall of the bedroom. As a result of pondering over this discrepancy he had actually woken up and got up and written down his dream.

The most puzzling type of dream, however, are the so-called lucid dreams in which the dreamer knows that he is dreaming. An entirely new dimension of consciousness opens up inside him. An experienced lucid dreamer can control his dreams and use them to overstep the bounds of time and space. Perhaps in this way he gains a better understanding of reality, for it would appear that real experience can only be gained by calling into question our limited capacity for perceiving the dimensions of time and space. Dreams which are controlled from within the dream must surely be the key here. Man must learn to dream, but above all he must learn to 'see'.

'Oh,' he said incredulously. 'I thought you had learned to use the darkness.'

'What can you use it for?' I asked.

He said the darkness – and he called it 'the darkness of the day' – was the best time to see. . .

The speakers are Don Juan, the Yaqui Indian, and his pupil, the writer Carlos Castaneda, to whom he explains that arranging dreams means having the situation in a dream firmly and pragmatically under control. Dreaming is as serious a matter as seeing or dying or anything else in this awesome, puzzling world.

'Let's have another look at our dreamer,' said the scientist to the journalist, glancing at the EEG recorder. 'As you know, we are already well on the way to recording dreams on magnetic tape. I need hardly enlarge on the fantastic prospects for the investigation of the human psyche which this opens up. We could create a dream library which would present the real, unvarnished history of mankind, with all its anxieties and needs, its hopes and desires, its weaknesses and strengths'.

'And reality too?' asked the journalist.

The researcher turned away impatiently.

'Reality?' he said, 'Reality? What the devil *is* reality?'

Bibliography

Aeppli, E. *Der Traum und seine Deutung.* Eugen Rentsch Verlag, 1973.

Alfvén, H. *Kosmologie und Antimaterie.* Frankfurt: Umschau Verlag, 1969.

Anderson, P. *Brain Wave.* New York: Ballantine Books, 1954.

Bateson, G. *Steps to an Ecology of Mind.* London: Paladin, 1973.

Becker, R. de. *The Understanding of Dreams,* transl. M. Heron. London: Allen & Unwin, 1968.

Berne, E. *Games People Play.* London: Deutsch, 1966; Harmondsworth: Penguin, 1968.

Blaker, Th. *A Pilgrimage of Dreams.* London: Turnstone Books, 1973.

Blofeld, I. *The Book of Change.* London: Allen & Unwin, 1968.

Bronowski, J. *The Ascent of Man.* London: BBC Publications, 1973.

Brown, J. A. C. *Freud and the Post-Freudians.* Harmondsworth: Penguin, 1976.

Buttlar, J. v. *Schneller als das Licht.* Düsseldorf: Econ Verlag, 1972.

Buttlar, J. v. *Reisen in die Ewigkeit.* Düsseldorf: Econ Verlag, 1973.

Buttlar, J. v. *Der Menschheitstraum.* Düsseldorf: Econ Verlag, 1975.

Caldin, M. *Three Corners to Nowhere.* New York: Bantam Books, 1975.

Calder, P. R. *Man and the Cosmos.* Harmondsworth: Penguin, 1970.

Caliger, L., and May, R. *Dreams and Symbols.* New York: Basic Books Inc., 1968.

Castaneda, C. *The Teachings of Don Juan: A Yaqui Way of Knowledge.* Harmondsworth: Penguin, 1970.

Castaneda, C. *A Separate Reality.* Harmondsworth: Penguin, 1973.

Castaneda, C. *Journey to Ixtlan.* Harmondsworth: Penguin, 1975.

Castaneda, C. *Tales of Power.* Harmondsworth: Penguin, 1976.

186

Colerus, E. *Vom Punkt zur vierten Dimension*. Reinbek bei Hamburg: Rowohlt, 1969.

Coxhead, D., and Hiller, S. *Dreams, Visions of the Night*. London: Thames & Hudson, 1976.

Delgado, J. M. R. *Physical Control of the Mind*. New York: Harper & Row, 1969.

Diamond,E.*The Science of Dreams*.London:Eyre & Spottiswoode,1962.

Ditfurth, H. v. *Der Geist fiel nicht vom Himmel*. Hamburg: Hoffmann und Campe, 1976.

Douglas, A. *Extra-Sensory Powers*. London: Gollancz, 1976.

Dunne, J.W. *An Experiment with Time*. London: Faber & Faber, 1927.

Eccles, J.C. (ed.). *Brain and Conscious Experience*. Berlin: Springer, 1966.

Einstein, A. *Mein Weltbild*. Amsterdam, 1934. (Translation in: *Ideas and Opinions*. London: Souvenir Press, 1973.)

Einstein, A. *The Meaning of Relativity*, 6th ed. London: Chapman & Hall, 1956.

Eliade, M. *Shamanism*. London: Routledge, 1964.

Eliade, M. *Yoga, Immortality and Freedom*. London: Routledge, 1958.

Faraday, A. *The Dream Game*. Harmondsworth: Penguin, 1976.

Faraday, A. *Dream Power*. London: Pan, 1973.

Flying Saucer Review: Case Histories. 1971.

Flugel, I.C. *Man, Morals and Society*. Harmondsworth: Penguin, 1962.

Foss, B.M. *New Horizons in Psychology*. Harmondsworth: Penguin, 1966.

Foulkes, D. *The Psychology of Sleep*. New York: Scribner, 1966.

Foulkes, S.H., and Anthony, E.J. *Group Psychotherapy*. Harmondsworth: Penguin, 1965.

Fowler, W., and Hoyle, F. *Nucleosynthesis in Massive Stars and Supernovae*. Chicago: University of Chicago Press, 1964.

Freud, S. *The Interpretation of Dreams*, ed. Angela Richards. Harmondsworth: Penguin, 1970.

Freud, S. *Selbstdarstellung*. Frankfurt: Fischer Taschenbuch, 1971.

Freud, S. *Totem and Taboo*. London: Routledge, 1960.

Freud, S. *Two Short Accounts of Psycho-Analysis*. Harmondsworth: Penguin, 1963.

Gamow, G. *Matter, Earth and Sky*, 2nd ed. Englewood Cliffs, NJ: Prentice-Hall, 1965.

Gilmor, D.S. (ed.). *Scientific Study of Unidentified Flying Objects*. New York: Bantam Books, 1969; London: Vision Press, 1970.

Gilgamesh, Epic of, ed. Nancy K. Sanders, Penguin, 1970.

Goffman, E. *Frame Analysis*. Harmondsworth: Penguin, 1975.

Gould, P., and White, R. *Mental Maps*. Harmondsworth: Penguin, 1974.

Govinda, Lama Anagarika. *The Way of the White Clouds*. London: Rider, 1973.

Govinda, Lama Anagarika. *Foundations of Tibetan Mysticism*. London: Rider, 1969.

Green, C. *Lucid Dreams*. London: Hamish Hamilton, 1968.

Green, C. *The Decline and Fall of Science*. London: Hamish Hamilton, 1976.

Grey, W. *The Living Brain*. Harmondsworth: Penguin, 1961.

Hall, C.S., and Nordby, V.J. *The Individual and his Dreams*, New American Library, 1972.

Hartmann, E.L. *The Functions of Sleep*. New Haven, Conn: Yale University Press, 1973.

Horney, K. *Self-Analysis*. London: Routledge, 1962.

Hoyle, F. *Galaxies, Nuclei and Quasars*. London: Heinemann, 1965.

Huxley, A. *The Doors of Perception, and Heaven and Hell*. Harmondsworth: Penguin, 1959.

Huxley, A. *Letters*, ed. G. Smith. London: Chatto & Windus, 1969.

Hynek, J.A. *The UFO Experience*. London: Corgi, 1974.

Jacobs, D.M. *The UFO Controversy in America*. Bloomington, Ind: Indiana University Press, 1975.

Jovanovic, U.J. *Schlaf und Traum*. Stuttgart: Gustav Fischer Verlag, 1974.

Jünger, E. *An der Zeitmauer*. Stuttgart: Ernst Klett Verlag, 1959.

Jung, C.G. *Modern Man in Search of a Soul*. London: Routledge, 1962.

Jung, C.G. *Memories, Dreams, Reflections*, transl. R. and C. Winston. London: Collins; Routledge, 1963.

Kacser, C. *Einführung in die Spezielle Relativitätstheorie*. Stuttgart: Berliner Union, 1970.

Keel, J.A. *Our Haunted Planet*. Sudbury: Neville Spearman, 1971.

Koch, E.R., and Kessler, W. *Am Ende ein neuer Mensch?* Stuttgart: Deutsche Verlags-Anstalt, 1974.

Koestler, A. *The Act of Creation*. London: Pan, 1966.

Lao Tzu. *Tao Te Ching*, transl. D.C. Lau. Harmondsworth: Penguin, 1969.

Lee, S.G.M., and Mayes, A.R. *Dreams and Dreaming*. Harmondsworth: Penguin, 1973.

Luce, G.G., and Segal, J. *Sleep and Dreams*. London: Panther, 1969

Marcuse, F.L. *Hypnosis*. Harmondsworth: Penguin, 1963.

McGuigan, F.J., and Schoonover, R.A. *The Psychophysiology of Thinking: Studies of Covert Processes*. New York: Academic Press, 1973.

Moody, R.A. jr. *Life after Life*. Covington, Ga: Mockingbird Books, 1975.

Moss, Th. *The Probability of the Impossible*. New York: Hawthorn Books, 1975.

Noone, R. *The Rape of the Dream People*. London: Hutchinson, 1972.

Ornstein, R. E. *On the Experience of Time*. Harmondsworth: Penguin, 1969.

Oswald, J. *Sleep*. Harmondsworth: Penguin, 1974.

Ouspensky, P.D. *In Search of the Miraculous*. London: Routledge, 1969.

Penfield, W. *The Excitable Cortex in Conscious Man*. Springfield, Ill: C.C. Thomas, 1958.

Pilgrim, V. E. *Der selbstbefriedigte Mensch*. Munich: Desch, 1975.

Rapaport, D. *Emotions and Memory*. New York: Science Editions Inc., 1961.

Reed, G. *The Psychology of Anomalous Experience*. London: Hutchinson, 1972.

Róheim, G. *The Gates of the Dream*. New York: International Universities Press, 1970.

Rose, St. *The Conscious Brain*. Harmondsworth: Penguin, 1976.

Ryle, G. *The Concept of Mind*. Harmondsworth: Penguin, 1976.

Sagan, C. *The Cosmic Connection*. London: Hodder & Stoughton, 1974.

Singer, J. L. *The Inner World of Daydreaming*. New York: Harper & Row, 1975.

Smith, A. *Powers of Mind*. London: W. H. Allen, 1976.

Schmidbauer, W. *Evolutionstheorie und Verhaltensforschung*. Hamburg: Hoffmann und Campe, 1974.

Stoyva, J. *Biofeedback and Self-Control*. Chicago, Ill: Aldine, 1972.

Tart, C. *Altered States of Consciousness*. New York: Wiley, 1969.

Taylor, E. F., and Wheeler, J. A. *Spacetime Physics*. San Francisco: W. H. Freeman & Co., 1966.

Taylor, J. G. *New Worlds in Physics*. London: Faber & Faber, 1974.

Thompson, R. F. *Physiological Psychology*. San Francisco: W. H. Freeman & Co., 1972.

Tomas, A. *Beyond the Time Barrier*. London: Sphere, 1974.

Torrey, E. F. *The Mind Game*. New York: Bantam Books, 1973.

Ullmann, M., Krippner, St., and Vaughan, A. *Dream Telepathy*. London: Turnstone Books, 1973.

Weil, A. *The Natural Mind*. Boston, Mass: Houghton Mifflin Co., 1972.

Widroe, H. *Human Behavior and Brain Function*. Chicago, Ill: C.C. Thomas, 1973.

Whitrow, G. J. *What is Time?* London: Thames & Hudson, 1972.

Wittgenstein, O.Graf. *Märchen, Träume, Schicksale*. Munich: Kindler, 1973.

Young, J. Z. *An Introduction to the Study of Man*. London: Oxford University Press, 1974.

Zubeck, J. P. *Sensory Deprivation.* Englewood Cliffs, NJ: Appleton-Century-Crofts, 1969.

Journals

Banquet, J. P. 'EEG and meditation', *Journal of Electroencephalography and Clinical Neurophysiology*, 33 (1972).

Barber, T. X. 'Physiological effects of hypnosis', *Psychological Bulletin*, 58 (1961).

Blackemore, C., and Cooper, J. F. 'Development of the brain depends on visual environment', *Nature*, 228 (1970).

Bogen, J. E. 'The other side of the brain', *Bulletin of L.A. Neurological Society*, 34 (1969).

Cooper, R. 'The psychology of boredom', *Science Journal*, 4, 2 (February 1968).

Fox, J. M. 'Schlafwandler', *Bild der Wissenschaft*, November 1976.

Franck, D. 'Gibt es wirklich keinen Aggressionstrieb?' *Umschau*, 10 (1976).

Hirsch, H. V. B., and Spinelli, D. N. 'Visual experience modifies distribution of horizontally and vertically oriented receptive fields in cats', *Science*, 168 (1970).

Keough, W. 'Life after death?', *The Sunday Bulletin*, 16 November 1975.

Krause-Weisser, F. 'Am Zabrastreifen Lauert der Tiger', *Stern*, 23 (1976).

Kuhn, H. 'Model consideration for the origin of Life', *Die Naturwissenschaften*, 63, 2 (February 1976).

Mitscherlich, A. 'Psychoanalyse ist Freud noch aktuell?', *Bild der Wissenschaft*, 12, 2 (August 1975).

Morgan, J. P. 'Psycho-pharmacology', *The Relevant Scientist*, 1. (November 1971).

Morgan, J. P. 'Psychotherapie. Der Streit der Schulen', *Bild der Wissenschaft*, 12, 9 (September 1975).

Soefeld, P. 'The benefits of boredom', *American Scientist*, 63 (1975).

Targ, R., and Putthof, H. 'Information transmission under conditions of sensory shielding', *Nature*, 252 (18 October 1974).

Wallace, A. F. C. 'Dreams and the wishes of the soul: a type of psychoanalytic theory among the seventeenth century Iroquois', *American Anthropologist*, 60 (1958), p. 234–48.

Whitrow, G. J. 'Time and timing', *Die Naturwissenschaften*, 64, 3 (March 1977).

Wilber, K. 'The ultimate state of consciousness', *Journal of Altered States of Consciousness*, 2, 3 (1976).

Index